Pets and Plants
in Miniature Gardens

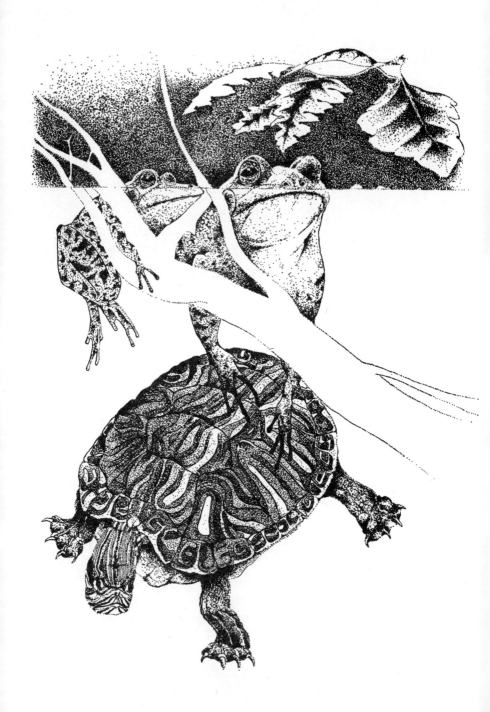

JACK KRAMER

Pets and Plants in Miniature Gardens

HOW TO CREATE WOODLAND, DESERT, BOG, OR TROPICAL SETTINGS

Animal Drawings by Cyrus Choy
Plant Drawings by Michael Valdez

DOUBLEDAY & COMPANY, INC. Garden City, New York

PHOTO CREDITS

Photographs by the Author: pages 15, 16, 17, 19, 21, 36 (below), 37, 40, 42, 43, 45, 46, 48, 49, 50, 53, 55, 94, 96, 97, 103, 111, 118, and 120–121.

Matthew Barr: 58, 63, 64, 65. 70, 72, 81, 91, and 92.

Merry Gardens: 36 (above).

Joyce R. Wilson: pages 28, 29, 33, 56, 57, 68–69, 77, 78–79, 84–85, 86, and 89.

ISBN: 0-385-08280-0
Library of Congress Catalog Card Number 72-89324
Copyright © 1973 by Jack Kramer

ACKNOWLEDGMENTS

Pet shop owners much like plant nursery people are invariably as interested in what you are doing as you are. They answer questions and give advice freely; to these folks (from California to Illinois to New York) I am forever indebted. Special gratitude goes to Dr. Ron Cauble of the Vivarium pet shop in Oakland, California, who guided me in the preparation of Chapter 4.

Special thanks go to the Steinhart Aquarium of San Francisco, California, for allowing us to photograph the Western newt, water skink, marbled newt, and snakes.

To various hobbyists throughout the country who shared their notes about vivariums with me, I owe special thanks. To the Fish and Game Departments of various states I owe a vote of respect for their splendid help about small pets and for the lists of endangered species and other printed matter they sent me.

Deep appreciation goes to my sister, Mrs. C. B. Sussman of Chicago, Illinois, for checking pet shops in her area about their stock. Finally, to the small boys in my neighborhood who volunteered their precious frogs and toads for our living gardens I will always be deeply touched.

CONTENTS

AUTHOR'S NOTE

In the course of working on this book I have kept many different kinds of reptiles and amphibians in glass gardens. The animals I suggest are those that were satisfactory for me and should by no means be considered a complete listing. Indeed, some of my failures may be your successes. Large animals were purposely deleted for I do not believe they belong in homes. I think few people would care for a two-foot lizard in the bathtub.

As much as possible I have avoided identification photos from museums. In essence, I tried to include only those plants and animals I personally worked with. Indeed, five living gardens still decorate my home and the animals in them seem content and robust after some eleven months.

This book is not meant to be a technical discussion on reptiles and amphibians, an enormous subject capably covered in many fine books. Some of these titles are listed in the Bibliography when animal identification and nomenclature are paramount.

What is here is an introduction to some common vivarium pets in simulated native habitats to make the creatures at home so they can live comfortably not as captives but as residents and at the same time to provide a piece of nature for viewing. I hope this book whets your imagination, piques your interest, and provides you with a better understanding of how animals and plants live together.

JACK KRAMER

Introduction: A Nature Study

The word *vivarium* is obscure, used long ago and since discarded. Yet, the vivarium — a case or container where small animals and plants live together — says a great deal. It tells you how plants and animals dwell harmoniously in a balanced environment. The living garden is planned and planted to represent an animal's natural habitat and the creatures are not merely curiosities in a cage. The pets are *at home* and watching them in their daily routine is a fascinating education.

These small gardens are planted to simulate natural scenes and they may have woodland, desert, bog, or tropical conditions. In each landscape certain plants thrive along with certain animals. A desert garden is home for interesting succulents and cacti and scampering lizards, tiny toads, perhaps a gecko. The bog garden is home for newts and salamanders who will earn their keep by eating insects and larvae that may infest plants. (With these animals at work there is no need for spraying plants with poisons.) In the woodland garden, lush green plants furnish a verdant background for delightful curious creatures like terrestrial newts and lively chameleons; some turtles, too, if plants are beyond their reach. In the vivarium we really see nature at work.

Pets, many of them, from baby iguanas to chameleons are available at most pet stores. If you have never encountered the world of the small critters there is adventure in store for you. Plants for living gardens may be ordered from suppliers or are at local florists in the house plant section. If you have never had a green thumb before here is an assured way of growing healthy plants. In simulated landscapes in containers they thrive, protected from drafts and fluctuating temperatures and inadequate humidity, which cause the demise of many house plants.

Selecting the proper plants for various environments and putting the appropriate animals in them is what this book is all about. We hope to show you the interrelationship of plants and animals, and if one of the critters becomes a pet — as invariably they do — this is a dividend of miniature gardens.

These small gardens are for everyone from eight to eighty years old. They are windows through which one can observe, learn, and understand more of the world around us.

1. Nature at Work

The glass case or Wardian case was introduced about 1836 by Nathaniel Ward, a surgeon in England. He wanted to make a study of the sphinx moth as it emerged from the chrysalis. Because the caterpillar burrows underground, Ward put the chrysalis in some moist earth in a bottle and covered the bottle with a stopper. Ward noticed that the heat of the day created moisture from the soil; this moisture condensed on the inner surface of the glass. A week later, as he was inspecting the insect, he saw tiny ferns and grasses growing in the bottle. In his excitement over the small plants, plants he had tried without success to grow in his yard, he forgot the moth, and thus the Wardian plant case was born.

The case was a boon to plantsmen, for it could be used for plants on their long voyages from foreign lands. But more importantly, perhaps, to indoor gardeners it provided a protected environment — a small conservatory where dozens of plants that previously were doomed to die on windowsills could be grown. A host of imitators designed cases, and eventually the terrarium evolved: a glass case with a cover, where plants could be grown not only under controlled conditions with little care but also in beautiful settings — a nature picture.

German records reveal that terrariums were used not only for propagation of choice plants but especially for housing exotic small creatures that could be observed for research.

The principle of a terrarium or a vivarium (in this book the names are used interchangeably) is a sound one. The case provides adequate humidity for plants and animals and protects them from drafts, fluctuating temperatures, and harmful pollution that may be in the atmosphere. Also, the plants and animals are easy to see and thus enjoy.

Today, in addition to glass containers, there are plexiglass and plastic ones. However, in these containers moisture condensing on the inside of the garden remains on the walls rather than dripping into the soil as it does in glass containers.

If properly planted and placed in a cool, light place, plants in a vivarium may not need water for months. But very few cases are this ideally arranged, so most (especially plexiglass) will need occasional watering to freshen plants and animals. Indeed, many lizards take water only from foliage and not from a dish.

Sometimes a vivarium may become overheated or too moist, in which case the cover should be removed so additional carbon dioxide can enter the garden and temperatures can cool. Just how often the lid should be lifted depends on the size of the case, how many plants and animals are in it, and where it is located. Observe, and, if sides of the vivarium are heavy with moisture, remove the lid for 20 or 30 minutes.

The addition of animal life makes the lilliputian garden a nature study. The animals help the plants, for they consume insects and larvae, and the plants provide a natural habitat for the animals.

Containers

What should you put your garden in? Almost any container with a cover or lid, from a cider jar to a decanter or a discarded aquarium, will do. My first gardens were in large peanut butter jars and vinegar jugs. Most gardens need a great deal of space; other scenes, with only one or two tiny

An aquarium is a popular container for living gardens. This one
has a screen cover and light reflector.

creatures and a few plants, can be at home in a large brandy
snifter. The size and number of animals will determine the
housing, as will the landscape you choose. Generally, I use
glass containers, except for one large hexagonal aquarium,
which is plexiglass; this material is clearer than standard
plastics and so far has worked well.

There are many kinds of glass containers. They may be
global, hexagonal, or octagonal shaped. The vivarium can be
a candy jar or a tobacco jar — all are adaptable. No matter
what housing you use, remember that for animals some type
of cover — screen or glass — will be necessary.

Although almost any transparent container can be used for
plants and animals, an aquarium is generally preferred. These
are available in sizes from 5 to 20 gallons, and they permit an
undistorted view of the garden.

The best aquariums have polished plate glass, enabling you
to view the scene without distortion, and the hardware is

Candy jars can be used for gardens too. After the animals are put in, a perforated cover is put on the jar.

stainless steel or aluminum. Plastic and plexiglass aquariums, sometimes called animal or specimen cases, are also available from suppliers. No matter which unit you choose, be sure it has no sharp edges inside or out that may harm animals. The aquariums with a metal cover over the top of the glass are convenient because you don't have to hunt glass covers and it lessens the possibility of glass slipping through your fingers and breaking.

Homemade terrariums are easy do-it-yourself projects, and you can build some elegant ones that will do any room proud. Years ago it was impossible to find glue to hold glass sides in place, so invariably there was leakage and a mess. I know; I struggled with discarded tanks many times. Now, new epoxies as strong as steel ensure a watertight container. (For more information see Chapter 3.)

Selecting the Environment

After you have the container for your living garden, think about the habitat you want to create. If you feel a little like God at this point, don't be too surprised; there is a joyous feeling in assembling this green world.

If you are fond of cacti and succulents, choose the desert landscape; if the woodland scene reminds you of childhood walks, duplicate this spring scene. If the boggy marsh has always fascinated you — and this is an easy garden to assemble — here is your chance to observe it close up.

This round glass cylinder makes an ideal home for plants and animals. A glass lid or screen cover is used for a top.

Once you have chosen the habitat, think about the plants and animals for it. Some plants — and animals too — need dryness and sun; others want moisture and shade. Even though you are creating the garden, nature will still dictate what goes into it. The chart at the end of this chapter tells you which animals are appropriate for what environment.

Animal Compatibility

When stocking the vivarium pay attention to what goes into it. If you just throw this and that together, you are liable to witness a cannibal feast that may be nature at work but is not what we are working toward. Animal compatibility is of prime importance. For example, frogs of the same size get along fine, but smaller species should not be put in with them or they will end up as dinner tidbits for the larger animals, since frogs think nothing of eating their own kind. And indeed they will, especially if they become very hungry.

Toads, on the other hand, are more selective in their diet and may be housed with chameleons or gopher tortoises. Indeed, toads are amenable creatures that will capture your fancy with their amusing antics. I had one that was a master of camouflage and seemed to delight in hiding from me. However, when my voice became loud or angry and I started away from the vivarium he would invariably appear. He was an avid attention-getter.

Lizards seem to prefer their own company and, although not overly sociable in the first few weeks with you, they will eventually accept your hospitality but still balk when strangers disturb them. Although I am fond of several lizards, I think the Madagascan gecko really captured my fancy. This is a perky little fellow that will invariably try to escape his home but never wanders far. He may occasionally nip your fingers too, but he never breaks skin. Newts and salamanders, more difficult to keep because they hide so much, will get

This charming woodland garden is in an inexpensive bubble bowl.

along with small frogs because neither has a voracious appetite.

Plants in the Miniature Garden

What plants go into the miniature garden? This depends on the landscape you choose to imitate. But no matter what garden you select, there are plants for it — some are at local nurseries, while others you must collect, but only with discretion (see Chapter 7), or buy from mail-order specialists. Remember, you are trying to duplicate nature, so make hills and valleys for interest, and use small stones for paths and some larger stones for animals to perch on as they do in their native habitat.

Plants for the garden should be removed from their pots; buy small plants in 2- to 3-inch containers. As you place plants, keep in mind the essentials of all good landscaping: scale, balance, and proportion. Don't use all green plants, but vary the picture with apple-green and gold-green and so forth. Use vertical and horizontal growing plants; pay attention to scale and balance.

Although you need enough plants in the garden to make it appear natural, do not crowd them, because plants need growing space and animals need room to move around comfortably.

Kinds of Gardens

The desert garden is naturally a place of contrasts: blazing hot in the day and cool at night. As the desert plants cool, moisture condenses on plants and rocks to serve as water for tiny animals. Plants for the desert are delightful anomalies of nature. You can choose from hundreds of bizarre cacti and succulents, such as gymnocalyciums, with leaves that seem carved from stone, or lobivias and parodias, with brightly colored flowers. Since the desert is too sandy for plant growth, leave plants in their pots.

The woodland environment is somewhat between the desert and bog garden; it is a re-creation of a forest floor, where it is moist and shady and where ferns, mosses, and lichens decorate the ground.

Toads and efts, skinks and fence lizards, wood frogs and tree frogs are good specimens to start with in the woodland garden. Do not have turtles in the woodland scene; they wreak havoc with plants. Provide some water, preferably in a separate container.

This garden needs bright light but little sun; the colorful

A desert garden is created in this glass punch bowl. With a screen top or glass lid with air holes it will make a fine home for desert animals.

cathedral of nature is always lush and verdant and an ideal home for the small critters mentioned. Use glass covers on top of the container to keep animals in and to help supply sufficient humidity for the plants.

The tropical setting is similar to the woodland scene, but there are differences in the choice of plants. And since more sun is welcome here there will be higher temperatures and brighter light, so choose such tropical house plants as episcias, with their flame-colored flowers, and small koelerias or smithianthas, always bright with bloom. For foliage plants select philodendrons and sansevierias (snake plants), pothos or pilea, or almost any warm-loving indoor plant.

Chameleons love this habitat, flashing color as they dart from plant to plant licking up moisture. Some frogs will prosper here too, but not salamanders, efts, or turtles; it will be too dry for them. You might try some toads, although they may find it too warm for comfort.

A bog garden is perhaps the most interesting landscape you can make. Here you can grow exotic mosses and lichens, ferns and orchids. Direct sun never reaches the ground in this garden, and there is a lush green picture. A water area is absolutely necessary for the animals and should be large enough for them to soak in. This is home for tiny skinks and tree frogs and nonaquatic newts and salamanders, but it is too moist for most toads. The bog garden is a veritable treasure house of nature, constantly alive and thoroughly engrossing.

The shoreline or water garden is a combination bog-and-water habitat. In fact, you must provide a barrier of wood or glass to separate one environment from the other. Bog plants such as horsetail, umbrella palm, and even miniature water iris can decorate this delightful scene. And the green frog, eft, and many kinds of salamanders and painted turtles will find this home to their liking.

Keep plants in their pots and at water level at the top of the pots for best results. Leave access from the gravel bog area into the water so animals can move back and forth.

For detailed instructions on putting together each kind of garden, see Chapter 5 for plant lists, and Chapter 4 for information on animals.

POPULAR VIVARIUM SPECIMENS

Specimens	Varieties (Common Name)	Best Habitats	Companions
Alligators	Crocodile	Shoreline	None, but same-sized brothers
	Caiman	Shoreline	None, but same-sized brothers
Frogs	Barking frog	Woodland	Same-sized frogs and toads; turtles
	Bullfrog	Bog	Same-sized frogs and toads; turtles
	Carpenter frog	Bog/woodland	Same-sized frogs and toads; turtles
	Florida chorus frog	Woodland	Same-sized frogs and toads; turtles
	Gray tree frog	Woodland	Same-sized frogs and toads; turtles
	Green tree frog	Shoreline	Same-sized frogs and toads; turtles
	Leopard frog	Woodland	Same-sized frogs and toads; turtles
	Pickerel frog	Bog	Toxic skin; keep alone
	Poison arrow frog	Tropical	Keep alone
	Ricord's frog	Tropical	Same-sized frogs and toads; turtles
	Spring peeper	Tropical	Same-sized frogs and toads; turtles
	Woodfrog	Woodland/tropical	Same-sized frogs and toads; turtles
Geckos	Banded gecko	Desert	Same-sized geckos; lizards
	Leaf-toed gecko	Tropical	Same-sized geckos; lizards
	Leopard gecko	Tropical/woodland	Same-sized geckos; lizards
	Madagascan day gecko	Woodland	Same-sized geckos; lizards
	Mediterranean gecko	Woodland	Same-sized geckos; lizards
	Moorish Gecko	Desert	Same-sized geckos; lizards
	Reef gecko	Woodland	Same-sized geckos; lizards
	Round-toed gecko	Tropical	Same-sized geckos; lizards
	Tokay gecko	Tropical	Same-sized geckos; lizards
	Fat-tail gecko	Desert	Same-sized geckos; lizards
	Frog-eyed gecko	Desert	Same-sized geckos; lizards
Lizards	Common basilisk	Tropical	Same-sized lizards; turtles
	Common chameleon	Tropical	Horned toads; gopher tortoises
	Desert horned toad (horned lizard)	Desert	Same-sized lizards; turtles
	Desert Iguana	Desert	Same-sized lizards; turtles
	Desert monitor	Desert	Same-sized lizards; turtles
	Eastern collared lizard	Desert/woodland	Keep alone

POPULAR VIVARIUM SPECIMENS

Specimens	Varieties (Common Name)	Best Habitats	Companions
	Fence lizard	Desert	Same-sized lizards; turtles
	Geckos (See Geckos)		
	Green iguana	Desert/tropical	Same-sized lizards; turtles
	Northern ground uta	Desert/tropical	Same-sized lizards; turtles
	Skinks (See Skinks)		
	Spiny-tailed iguana	Desert	Same-sized lizards; turtles
Newts (See Salamanders)			
Salamanders	Japanese newt	Woodland/bog	Same-sized salamanders; small frogs
	Marbled salamander	Woodland	Same-sized salamanders; small frogs
	Mole salamander	Bog	Same-sized salamanders; small frogs
	Red-backed salamander	Woodland	Same-sized salamanders; small frogs
	Red salamander	Woodland/bog	Same-sized salamanders; small frogs
	Red-spotted newt	Woodland/bog	Same-sized salamanders; small frogs
	Tiger salamander	Woodland/bog	Same-sized salamanders; small frogs
	Western newt	Woodland/bog	Same-sized salamanders; small frogs
	Zigzag salamander	Woodland	Same-sized salamanders; small frogs
Skinks	Common Western Skink	Woodland	Small lizards
	Four-striped skink		
	Four-striped skink	Woodland	Small lizards
	Mountain skink	Woodland	Small lizards
	Short-lined skink	Woodland	Small lizards
	Striped red-tailed skink	Woodland	Small lizards
	Water skink	Bog	
Toads	American toad	Woodland	Same-sized toads or lizards
	Little green toad	Tropical	Same-sized toads or lizards
	Oak toad	Woodland/tropical	Same-sized toads or lizards

POPULAR VIVARIUM SPECIMENS

Specimens	Varieties (Common Name)	Best Habitats	Companions
	Southern toad	Woodland/bog	Same-sized toads or lizards
	Spadefoot toad	Tropical	Same-sized toads or lizards
	Western toad	Woodland/bog	Same-sized toads or lizards
	Woodhouse's toad	Woodland/bog	Same-sized toads or lizards
Turtles	Black pond turtle	Tropical	Lizards; other turtles
	Box turtle	Woodland	Lizards; other turtles
	European pond turtle	Shoreline	Lizards; other turtles
	Gopher tortoise	Desert/tropical	Lizards; other turtles
	Greek tortoise	Woodland/desert	Lizards; other turtles
	Herman's tortoise	Desert	Lizards; other turtles
	Indian star tortoise	Desert/tropical	Lizards; other turtles
	Malayan leaf turtle	Tropical	Lizards; other turtles
	Mobile turtle	Shoreline	Lizards; other turtles
	Mud turtle	Shoreline	Lizards; other turtles
	Musk turtle	Shoreline	Lizards; other turtles
	Northern diamondback terrapin	Shoreline	Lizards; other turtles
	Painted turtle	Shoreline	Lizards; other turtles
	Red-eared turtle	Bog/shoreline	Lizards; other turtles
	Red-footed tortoise	Tropical	Lizards; other turtles
	Sawback turtle	Tropical	Lizards; other turtles
	Spotted turtle	Bog/woodland	Lizards; other turtles
	Wood turtle	Woodland	Lizards; other turtles

VIVARIUM CONDITIONS

Type of garden	Temperature range, °F		Light requirement
Desert	80–90 day	60–65 night	Sun
Tropical	75–85 day	60–65 night	Some sun
Woodland	65–75 day	55–60 night	Bright; no sun
Bog	75–80 day	60–65 night	Shade
Shoreline	75–85 day	65–70 night	Sun; shade

2. How to Get Started

No matter what kind of container you choose or which native habitat you decide to duplicate in miniature, you want to choose alert animals and healthy plants. It is important to know something about reptiles and amphibians and their habits so you can care for them intelligently, and it is also prudent to have some basic knowledge about the plants that are part of your pets' home.

Observation is the key to success with animals and plants. Before you buy pets at local shops, watch them for fifteen or thirty minutes to see if they are alert. Just don't choose a creature because of color or shape. Ask the shop owner the real name of the reptile or amphibian, what it eats, where it comes from, and how warm it should be kept. If the clerk cannot give you this information don't buy the animal; too many reptiles and amphibians die each year because people who buy them do not know enough about them. Also visit the local aquarium (if in a large city) to really see reptiles and amphibians. Ask questions; if you know what you are doing before you start, things will be easier later.

Select plants in tiptop shape, with fresh green leaves and strong stems. It takes but a few minutes to pick up a plant and inspect it. Again, ask questions: where the plant comes from, its right name, and so forth. Then you have some idea of the kind of environment is needs to grow and can check horticultural manuals for further information.

Selecting Animals

Selection of lizards and amphibians varies, depending on the pet shop. Some have large selections that include foreign exotic geckos and salamanders (these are more colorful than native species). Other shops stock only a few favorites like chameleons, frogs, and iguanas. Some pets cost as little as fifty cents, while others, such as the Pakistani lizards, may be ten dollars a pair.

As mentioned, before you buy, observe the creatures for a while. Are they alert? Do they respond to a tap on the glass? Lethargy in an animal usually indicates that it is in poor health (unless in hibernation state). Check the eyes closely. For example, geckos whose eyes have a sunken appearance are apt to be suffering from dehydration. Check lizards' feet to be sure there are no digits missing, and observe their tails; those with the stoutest tail are likely to be the healthiest. The skin of the lizard is another sign of his health. If it is shedding it looks repulsive, like it is covered with torn white tissue paper. If the skin is peeling off in large- or medium-sized patches, the lizard is apt to be in good health, but if the skin is ragged with large cracks, avoid the animal.

Let me remind you once again that once you decide on your pet, find out what he eats before you buy him. If you can supply food and a reasonably appropriate habitat for the creature you have a good chance of keeping him alive and contented. Otherwise it is a waste of money and cruel to the animals. For collecting your own animals see Chapter 7.

About Lizards

Some lizards are insectivorous and are active during the day; at night they remain hidden under rocks and in cracks. (An exception are geckos who are active at night.) On dull days many lizards will usually stay hidden and not appear

This amenable fence lizard does not mind being handled; he's alert, fat, and healthy.

in the terrarium at all. Day lizards reach a peak of activity about noon, hide during the middle of the day, and appear about four o'clock, quite chipper and demanding attention (but much less active than at morning).

Reptiles are largely dependent upon external sources of heat to help them maintain proper body temperature. Since nature provides a great temperature range, animals must have some means of adjustment to survive, and they do, simply by retiring into rocks and crevices under the surface of the ground to avoid high or low temperatures.

Most lizards are dark colored in low temperatures and light colored at high temperatures. This color regulation prevents overheating, since maximum heat absorption occurs in the

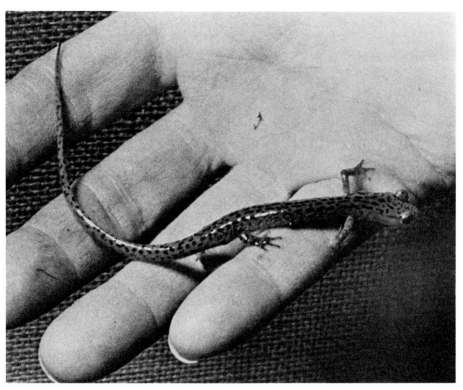

Tiny and curious, a cave salamander clings to the author's hand. He would much rather be in his home where he can hide.

presence of a dark color, such as is exhibited in uniform pigment. Although color change probably has its origin in heat control, some lizards also change colors during various emotional states.

Many desert reptiles acquire water from or by chemical changes of the food they have eaten, rather than by drinking. Nondesert lizards, however, *must* have water, if infrequently. Some lizards refuse water in dishes (chameleons, for example) and only take droplets from foliage or sides of glass cases. Drinking water does not aid in regulation of body temperature since reptiles do not sweat and, as noted, desert species do not drink water.

Do not be disturbed if you don't see your lizards too often;

burrowing is one of their characteristics. Because most lizards construct a burrow for their eggs (except geckos), the practice is quite common.

Rarely do lizards bite people. Species with large claws can inflict a wound, and then only if they are provoked. Generally, lizards and all animals mentioned in this book do not exceed eight inches in length. However, these small lizards can grab hold of a finger, but they will rarely puncture the skin. Let the lizard hang on; do not pull him from your finger or you will injure both him and yourself. Simply lower your hand over the vivarium and he will let go.

Fence lizards (swifts) and horned lizards (toads) are the most popular of the desert reptiles because they are robust and prosper well in captivity. They make excellent pets and live a long time in a desert environment with proper feeding and care.

Collared lizards are beautiful animals, primarily carnivorous, and amenable pets in a semidesert vivarium. They are alert, curious, and provide hours of interest; they are commonly available too at low prices. Keep them with their own species or with animals the same size since they do have cannibalistic tendencies. Collared lizards thrive on grasshoppers, crickets, and meal worms.

Geckos are a group of handsome lizards that are nocturnal rather than diurnal. There are several species, although some, like the Moorish geckos and the round-toed geckos, are more handsome than others. The banded geckos of the southwestern United States are also popular because of their colorful patterns. Avoid the Tokay geckos because they do bite, but on the other hand, the Indian geckos are quite gentle. Madagascan day geckos are beautiful, and frog-eyed geckos are invariably cute.

The American chameleons (anoles) have been hobbyist's favorites for many years. These interesting small lizards are not true chameleons, which are quite different animals and

Tree frog.

not at all as handsome. The anoles are scampering creatures, curious and full of mischief. They are content in a tropical vivarium and are excellent pets.

Iguanas invariably make poor pets, and the baby ones being sold, pretty though they may be with their chartreuse coloring, are not meant for the home terrarium. They are difficult to keep, eat plants, and rarely live more than six months. And if they do they grow so large they become more of a burden than a blessing.

Alligators, crocodiles, and caymans are three types of aquatic reptiles; generally all are referred to as alligators, yet the creatures sold in pet shops are invariably caymans. For the most part, these animals grow quickly and soon become too large for the terrariums. Furthermore, they require special food, invariably bite, and are generally not good pets; however, the experienced person can try them.

Other Creatures

The turtles sold in virtually every pet shop are generally red-eared sliders or map turtles, although other kinds are sold too. In a proper terrarium turtles make fine pets; in unsuitable quarters, such as a jar, they die soon.

Frogs and toads are amphibians that lack scales and must be kept in damp places. They do well in a woodland scene or shoreline terrarium. Small frogs are fine for the vivarium, but the larger ones, such as the bullfrogs, need live mice, and this feeding procedure really should not be practiced in a home. Small toads, however, make excellent pets.

Salamanders are amphibians and like a damp woodland scene. There are many species that make fascinating pets, such as the Japanese red-bellied salamander (also called newt) and the Eastern spotted salamander.

Skinks are curious creatures, but these reptiles hide so much of the time they make poor pets.

Snakes are frequently kept in vivariums because most (for

These Mexican toads are robust creatures and make fine pets even though they always seem to be looking at you rather than you looking at them.

Baby iguanas are perky fellows, agile, and fun to watch; however, they do not make very good pets because they eat plants and eventually become quite large.

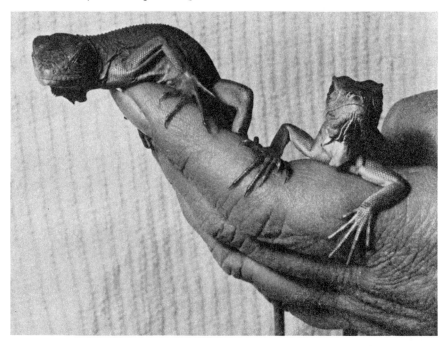

Fence lizards

example, the garter snake and smaller species) make good pets, but in this book we have touched only lightly on this category. I must admit this was by choice, not space. I am not immensely fond of snakes, and since I decided to write about only those animals I personally kept myself, few are included.

Setting up a proper environment for your pet is simple and costs but a few pennies more than keeping them in bare cages. In a simulated scene animals live longer and are happier, and you will learn a lot about how plants and animals live together. Thus, in the long run everyone benefits.

Selecting Plants

There are hundreds of small plants for the vivarium, and choice, as mentioned, depends on the scene you want to duplicate. These gardens are discussed fully in Chapter 5. In the meantime, some basic knowledge of small plants and their care will help you help your pets.

Although miniature plants to eight inches in height are best for vivariums, almost any house plant can be used in its young stage. Seedlings of popular house plants are available at most florists and nurseries in 2- or 3-inch pots, ready to be planted in the vivarium. Arrangement and choice of plant varies depending on the animals and the scene chosen.

There are basically four groups of plants you should select from: (1) such succulents and cacti as gymnocalycium and haworthia, (2) tropical plants — and these include most house plants — such as begonias and African violets, (3) plants that like a bog situation (for example, marsh marigolds), and (4) native plants such as partridge berry and wild orchids. All these plants are at florists in the house-plant section or are available from mail-order suppliers. In addition, you should have mosses, lichens, and ferns for the woodland and bog gardens, for these plants are the floor of the forest and more interesting plants are difficult to find. Very natural scenes

Select plants in small pots for vivarium planting. This is a group of Pileas.

Selaginellas are excellent vivarium plants. The species on the left is dark green; the other, a lighter green.

Mosses or ground covers are purchased in chunks from nurseries. Irish moss, Baby's tears, and several others are excellent to clothe a vivarium floor.

This is a tiny-leafed ground cover perfect for living gardens.

can be created with delicate ferns scattered around and lustrous green carpets of mosses.

Along with the true miniature plants you should use seedlings of standard plants. *Ficus pumila* (the climbing fig) has delightful button green leaves, puts out disks that cling to glass, and grows easily in terrariums. Small-leaved English ivy (*Hedera helix*) is always welcome but often becomes too rampant in growth. However, Pellionia species grow slowly, and *Tradescantia fluminensis* (wandering Jew), with its maroon-streaked or plain green leaves, is suitable. Fittonias are especially handsome with their velvety leaves with pink veins, and Marantas and Malpighias are equally attractive.

Seedling trees are other candidates for your lilliputian garden. These include Hemlock (Tsuga), Yew (Taxus), and Spruce. Seedling palms such as *Cocos weddelliana* and *Phoenix roebelenii* are always welcome, if somewhat large, but since they grow slowly, they are satisfactory.

Even though you want plants in the setting, remember that you must have space for animals too, so use plants judiciously. Because lizards and especially chameleons love to clamber over vegetation, be sure to choose plants with strong stems and tolerant foliage. Do not be too upset if you have to occasionally replace plants that may be uprooted. If you keep turtles (they love to eat foliage), remember to put plants above their reach. Suspending plants from the top of the aquarium creates a hanging garden and solves this problem. For plant lists see Chapter 5.

3. Preparing the Terrarium

The new home for your small creatures should be a place where *they feel at home*. Pet shop cases are unsightly and hardly fair to the creatures for they are not a fit place to live. Of course, the shop owners are in business to sell animals, not to put them in pretty surroundings. Yet the vivarium is, as we mentioned, more than a home for the animals; it is also a segment of nature with plants and soil, a living green picture where we can enjoy the creatures and have the fascination of seeing them in daily activity. In a balanced environment animals and plants give the viewer a natural picture.

The standard aquarium is perhaps the most popular container for the vivarium but *certainly not the only kind*. Its rectangular shape limits landscapes, whereas spectacular scenes can be made in circular and free-form glass containers, bubble bowls, unique glass and plexiglass containers, and so on. No matter what kind of container you use, the planting plan changes depending on the animals housed and the shape and size of the glass garden.

Containers

The first consideration in selecting a container is to choose one you can see through and that is large enough to accommodate the animals you intend to have as pets. Small containers like brandy snifters and candy vases are not suitable

A plexiglass container is being planted as a woodland garden. Low-growing mosses and native plants have been used exclusively. This container comes with a sealed attached cover with a hand hole, so planting is no problem.

for lizards, geckos, turtles, or frogs because these living creatures need space, not a prison. Better put a ladybug or a cricket in a small glass bowl, not animals.

Containers are sold by size (16×20, 20×24) and also by liquid capacity (5, 10, 15 gallons) since many are meant to be used as aquariums. The common aquarium is well known and needs little description, but the specimen case is better because the height of the case is increased by a slanting glass on top of the normal flat glass front. *Remember that with any container a top is necessary so animals do not wander.* It's disconcerting to find animals watching you rather than you watching the animals.

The small animal cage sold in pet shops is generally an aquarium type fitted with a perforated metal cover that shuts securely. Sometimes a fluorescent-light-tube fixture is incorporated into the design. With other containers you have to devise your own cover, which can be simply hard-ware cloth (wire mesh at hardware stores) weighted down at the ends or glass covers (use $\frac{3}{16}$-inch-thick glass) cut 1 inch larger than the vivarium and drilled with several $\frac{1}{4}$-inch air holes (or propped on wooden blocks). For example, if the container is 12 inches in diameter, have a piece of glass 13 inches in diameter cut for the top with six air holes ($\frac{1}{4}$ inch) drilled in designated places. (Perforated metal tops in three sizes are also now available at pet shops.)

The specific containers I use that are satisfactory are a 12×16-inch cylinder, a 16×8-inch container, and a 14-inch glass bowl; the latter makes exceptionally fine housing for turtles. These hand-blown glass containers do not have metal channels or corners, giving an undistorted view of the garden, and one-piece glass gardens eliminate any chance of leaks. You have to search for such unusual containers, but it is worth the effort because they are a welcome relief from the usual rectangular aquariums. (I found them in gift shops and boutiques.)

Recently at pet shops plexiglass aquariums have appeared. The one I purchased has a 12-gallon capacity and is 14 inches across and 24 inches high. It is an ideal home for pets and plants because there are no metal flanges to obscure the view and the one-piece construction makes a strong unit. Further-more, the hexagonal shape is pleasing to the eye. The plexi-

This is the start of a desert garden. Sand and gravel have been put in place and ledges set in position. Next, plants will be added in the rear of the vivarium and the front area will be left open for animals.

glass container is also available in a 25-gallon size, which is large enough for several animals and many plants and makes a stunning picture when properly landscaped.

Do not use glass containers like dome gardens and mushroom-shaped terrariums; the cover fits on top of a planting bowl, and the animals invariably escape when you clean the garden. Bubble bowls and other larger glass vases and jars that have ample openings can be used provided you devise a cover of glass or hardware cloth for them.

Glass is the ideal choice for a container, but, as mentioned, plexiglass is suitable too. However, avoid inferior plastics; view is always cloudy, and surfaces become slimy with algae, making cleaning difficult.

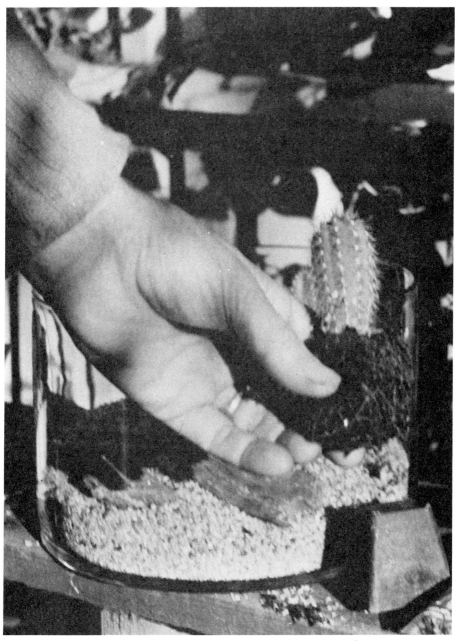

When you put plants in the desert garden, leave some soil around the roots.

Beware of thick or colored glass because view will be disturbingly distorted. The popular 5- and 15-gallon water bottles used for terrariums have been improved in glass quality but still leave much to be desired. You might also want to make your own container from glass panes or plexiglass sheets. Use 3/16-inch glass or 1/4-inch plexiglass. Today, with new epoxies, construction is easy. It is more a matter of patience and experience than materials, as it was in the past.

Design and Arrangement

Approach the housing for plants and animals as if it were a landscape. Indeed, what you are trying to accomplish is a scene from nature. A flat terrain is rarely interesting. Remember what captured your fancy on woodland walks? It was generally a rolling, hilly situation, a particular rock formation, or perhaps a ravine bordered with tall reeds. This perfect balance of beauty is what you want to duplicate in your terrariums in miniature. Many common house plants can act as trees; mosses and lichens provide a touch of authenticity, and creeping plants like *Pilea repens* and *Pellionia daveaunana* provide lush green looks common to woodsy scenes. The choice is vast, but always remember that you must use plants that will grow together and will be in keeping with the animals you have planned for the scene.

Small geckos and other lizards need space to explore and hide, so an area of the terrarium should have a level uncluttered design, another area some rocks on chunks of wood. Generally, this is in the front of the tank, or in round containers it can be front and back for viewing from two sides.

If you are using rectangular containers, start in a rear corner and create a small hill, making dynamic use of line and rhythm combined with color texture and structural forms. To build the corner arrangement use small pieces of slate or other flat porous material; even broken pieces of clay pots will do. Set these pieces in layers on a small bed of soil

This woodland garden has just been started. A vertical stone has been put in place surrounded by ground cover. Plants (in small pots at left) will frame the stone, and once again the front area will be left open for view.

and then cover the entire projection with soil and sphagnum. Leave the edges of the slate or pot pieces showing here and there to simulate a natural-rock outcropping.

With the round- or free-shaped glass container, use a focal point by building islands slightly to the left or right. Construct the islands in the same manner as the corner arrangements for aquariums. Balance the scene with smaller islands so proportion and scale are kept within harmony, and always remember to leave enough space for the animals.

Whether you use free-form cylinders or rectangular housings, incorporate small attractive bonsai-type branches, and use handsome rocks and stones so animals have places to hide

The finished woodland garden with four ¼-inch holes in the glass lid.

or to sit on when basking in the sun. Create a lilliputian world of greenery pleasing to the eye and useful for the creatures.

The following principles govern the design of the garden, although gardens may be of many different themes:

1. Materials like stone, rock, or gravel should be repeated more than twice so there is a harmony in the garden.

2. Although you want many plants, do not make a crowded jungle; use restraint and good taste.

3. Make all parts of the design in pleasing proportion.

You will be amazed at the many different landscapes you can assemble in one small container. The mood can be formal, informal, simple, elegant, natural, and so forth; design is governed only by your imagination.

Setting Up the Vivarium

After you have selected the container and its design, start the planting and landscaping plan. Take your time in creating the perfect picture for viewing and for the creature. Soil base and soils must be carefully considered, and choice of plants is vital if you want gardens to last for years rather than a few weeks.

Be sure the container is absolutely clean when you start; do not use commercial window-cleaning preparations. Some contain chemicals that be harmful to plants or animals. Use a soapy-water solution to clean the glass, and then rinse thoroughly several times. Or, to get the container sparkling clean, buy some carborundum powder (available at hardware stores), mix it with a little water, smear on glass, let dry, and then wash glass; rinse thoroughly. Do not use any sink cleansers that contain abrasives because they can scratch glass or plastic.

When the container is clean, insert a bed of pea gravel (use about an inch). Over this sprinkle bits of charcoal

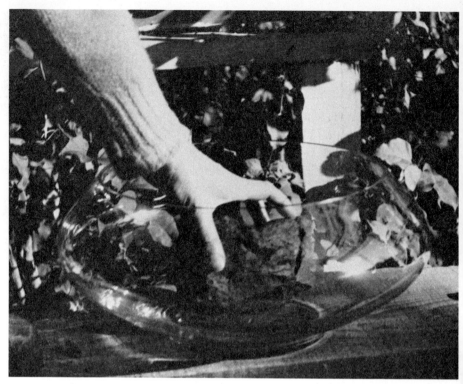

A desert garden being prepared for animals. A large stone is set in place for a focal point.

granules (sold in packages at nurseries) where you want plantings. Remember to leave some bare soil areas for animals so they can scamper about without disturbing plants and so you can watch them. Then spread a rich porous soil in place to about 3 to 5 inches, depending on the height of the container. The mix can be leaf mold and sand, a peat-sand-gravel-leaf mold medium, or whatever you have in your garden or flowerpots. The soil should neither cake nor fall apart readily; it should be porous and mealy like a baked potato. But no matter what mix you use, be sure to place small gravel at the bottom of the tank to provide good drainage.

To make desert scenes you need a sandy soil base; this is explained in Chapter 5. Sterilized soil, which is always recommended for house plants, need not concern you. It is used

Plants with soil at the roots are being placed around the stone. Before this, a sand base was put in place.

to kill all insects and insect eggs and harmful bacteria, but with lizards and/or frogs and toads in your garden you can forget about sterilizing soil or using chemicals to combat insects; lizards love to eat insects.

After the base is in place, install the central focus. If it is a ledge of rocks, affix it carefully in a pleasing pattern. If you use small tree branches, place them carefully to form a setting similar to what you see in nature.

Once all materials are in place, place and trim plants so they are attractive. Remove large or limp leaves, any frond that touches the glass or obscures the main vision, any stalk or foliage that is not pleasing. This miniature scene should be perfect in every detail for it will be under constant scrutiny. Cut stems and stalks at the base so there is no possibility of

Finishing the desert garden by adding small grains of colored sand.

decay, and then dust the wounds with powdered charcoal to check mold.

Dust off leaves with an artist's paintbrush, and mist the soil lightly in a uniform pattern. Don't just dump water into the terrarium; it will splash soil over everything. Put small creatures into their new home, and set the cover (wire or glass) in place.

Watch the vivarium closely for a few days to see how animals are reacting and whether they appear listless or active in their new setting. This will indicate if all is well or if something is awry.

Place the vivarium in its permanent place — sun or shade depending on the scene and temperatures needed for plants and animals. If heat is needed, use a canopy fixture with a 15-watt light bulb, or put the vivarium under an ordinary reading lamp left on for the night.

4. The Pets

Choosing the animals for your gardens is always difficult because there are so many beguiling creatures, and each group — reptiles, amphibians — seem to have their own endearing idiosyncrasies. Whether you select animals for their colors, shapes, or habits, or just because they happen to appeal to you, don't set up too many gardens at once. Start with one, observe and enjoy it, and then go on to other, more elaborate scenes and more exotic animals.

Creatures sold at pet shops are placed in small cardboard boxes. Don't keep the animals in the car too long, and be sure they don't escape en route to their new home. Furthermore, be sure they are warm if it is winter — set them near but not on the car heater. And remember: once you purchase the animals, their homes should be waiting for them and not vice versa. (To collect your own animals and plants see Chapter 7.)

Chameleons

These are so popular that they deserve a listing of their own. Chameleons are amazing little creatures that make good pets; you will become fond of them in little time. Chameleons are an endless cycle of energy as they romp about tree limbs, chase insects, and change color. However, the color change is

Chamelon (anole)

This chamelon — really from the genus Anolis — peers back at the photographer.

really not drastic; generally chameleons can master only two colors: brown and green.

These small pets want attention, and after a time will let you rub their throats and even feed them. The chameleon you buy is an American species known as *Anolis carolinensis*. It is native to North Carolina and surrounding regions, as far east as Florida and as far west as the Rio Grande River. Your pet is not a true chameleon but is somewhat related to the true species of Madagascar and some parts of Africa. He is long and sleek, with a scaly body, and has four legs, a graceful long tail, and tiny sharp teeth. The chameleon uses his tail for balancing while running and leaping, so do not pick him up by the tail because it is likely to come off. Nature intended the tail to be brittle for it is the first part an enemy would attack and thus is part of a chameleon's defense. If you do break the tail, don't panic, because in a short time a new tail (albeit not so handsome) will grow.

A chameleon has five toes on each foot, with long claws, so he is naturally an excellent climber, and his legs are stocky for quick pursuit. He has ears on each side of his head, a bit behind the eyes, and a good sense of hearing. His eyes act independently of each other, and he can see different things on each side at the same time.

Chameleons stalk insects just as a cat stalks a mouse; small grasshoppers, mosquitoes, and houseflies are chameleons' diet. They also eat caterpillars, fruit flies, and, in the winter, meal-worms. Don't force your pet to eat; he can go weeks without food with no harm. In summer, catch live insects for him (he will not eat dead ones). In winter, pet shops sell grubs and mealworms. Put food in front of him where he can see it and feed by day, not at night.

Most chameleons from pet shops die in a few weeks because people give them water in a dish, which they won't touch. Yet chameleons need a good quantity of water if they are to survive. They drink water and dew that accumulates on *leaves,* so be sure to sprinkle plants generously in the vivar-ium. Do not confuse the common chameleon with the au-thentic ones from Africa. Those fellows look entirely different and are difficult to keep, needing 90°F heat and special care. Furthermore, they are expensive, and the one we had, al-though given excellent care, did not survive a month.

The woodland or tropical garden is the place for your chameleon (see Chapter 5).

Frogs and Toads

This is a varied group of likable comedians with short bodies and long limbs. They are found in temperate and tropical habitats. Just what kind of frog you get depends on

Tree frogs are charming pets and are right at home on this branch.

These green tree frogs are as curious about you as you are about them.

the pet store you frequent, or, if you collect them yourself, where you live.

Frogs and toads are amphibians (the word means double life) because they spend part of their life on land and part of their life in water.

Generally these pets are harmless and will not bite. Toads have no teeth, but frogs do and swallow their food in one piece; both are alert, agile, and delightful creatures, with their tiny little hands always fascinating to watch.

A toad's skin is perfectly dry, while a frog's is wet. The toad's legs are powerful, with five toes on the front and the back legs, enabling him to make long leaps. His tongue is long and sticky, and he can thrust it out swiftly to snare an insect. Toads don't have many protective devices to help them elude enemies, but they can change color to blend with

Mexican toads gather at the glass to see who's there.

their surroundings, and they have the ability to play possum when in danger.

The frog's body is slimmer than the toad's, and he does not have warts; he is slippery to the touch. His eyes are quite handsome, and his body is brightly colored, in contrast with a toad's, which is generally dull in color. The frog's teeth are set into horny jaws, and when you watch him eat you will note he takes chunks of food.

The home for frogs and toads should be somewhat large and sufficiently heated. Usually a hood or canopy light that doesn't use too much electricity and still supplies a good amount of heat is suitable. Include an area of water in the vivarium. The woodland terrarium is fine for toads; a shore-line terrarium is good for some frogs, but others need a tropical or woodland habitat with water.

A gathering of the clan. These leopard frogs are discussing weighty matters.

What do these creatures eat? Practically anything that moves, so food must be given live. Grasshoppers, cockroaches, and worms are all ideal fare for the toad and frog. Plant insects are also fine in the diet; indeed, a frog or toad will keep plants meticulously clean and love it in the bargain.

Tree frogs are delightful critters, highly colored and diminutive in size. The toes on their feet have little round pads that secrete a sticky substance, enabling them to cling to slippery surfaces. They are quite active and dislike captivity but eventually become amusing pets. Tree frogs are mainly arboreal and belong to the family Hylidae, while cricket frogs (Acris) and chorus frogs (Pseudoacris) spend most of their time on the ground. These amphibians need a woodland or tropical habitat.

Bull frog

Ideal frogs and toads for the vivarium include:

Florida chorus frog (*Pseudoacris nigrita verrucosa*). Prefers prairie lands and grassy habitats; only 2 inches; great leaper.

Little green toad (*Bufo debilis*). Inhabits semiarid grassy lands. Green with black spots on back.

Ornate chorus frog (*Pseudoacris ornata*). Lively and active and likes dry places, so he is at home in the tropical habitat. Diminutive; excellent jumper.

Oak toad (*Bufo quercicus*). Only 1 inch long, and a delight to have in a vivarium. Likes warmth.

Ricord's frog (*Eleutherodactylus ricordii planirostris*). Only 1½ inches long, with striped and mottled colors. This frog prefers a warm and humid tropical garden.

Rana is the genus name for true frogs and includes hundreds of species. Ranas are generally not good for terrariums because they hop around so much. Ranas include:

Bullfrog (*Rana catesbeiana*). Large and never really makes a good pet unless he has ample space to hop around.

Carpenter frog (*R. virgatipes*). Grows to 3 inches and is at home in wooded or bog situations.

Pickerel frog (*R. palustris*). Abundant in central New York; generally hibernates in winter and is not a good pet.

Wood frog (*R. sylvatica sylvatica*). Grows to 4 inches and sometimes adjusts to captivity; prefers a tropical or wooded habitat.

Toads (Bufo) are widely distributed throughout the United States with seventeen species in North America. Here are some we have kept as pets and they make fine terrarium subjects:

American toad (*B. americanus americanus*). This is the little fellow you are most apt to find in your garden. Excellent pet for woodland vivarium.

Southern toad (*B. terrestris*). Frequently found in pet shops. Varies in color from red or gray to black.

Spadefoot toad (*Scaphiopus holbrookii holbrookii*). Grows from 2 to 3 inches, has smooth moist skin and one large black digging tubercle on each hind foot. Spadefoots are nocturnal and burrowers, and some species can endure warm waterless areas.

Western toad (*Bufo cognatus*). A common garden toad and a veritable insect-eating machine.

Woodhouse's toad (*B. woodhousii*). Can get along in almost any environment where there is some water. Grows to 4¾ inches.

Tree frogs (Hylidae) are mainly arboreal. These are delightful creatures for the woodland garden, where thay will scamper and play completely at home. (They have adhesive pads at the tips of their digits so they can climb and dart about with ease.) The exception is the terrestrial cricket frog (*Acris gryllus*), which is not a very good climber. The Hyla frogs like a moist woodsy terrarium and include:

Green tree frog (*Hyla cinerea cinerea*). Never grows more than 2½ inches and is always fascinating to watch.
Parific tree frog (*H. regilla*). Wee and lively and adjusts readily to a vivarium.
Spring peeper (*H. crucifer crucifer*). Popular, a diminutive clown, and an excellent insect eater.
Western tree frog (*H. versicolor chrysocelis*). Another suitable subject for the woodland garden.

Tiger salamander

The Japanese newt is a curious fellow, generally quite alert and a real acrobat.

Salamanders and Newts

Many people confuse salamanders with lizards, but there are noticeable differences. A lizard's skin is covered with tiny scales and is quite hard and dry, while a salamander's (also called a newt; a newt is a particular kind of salamander) is slightly moist and soft to the touch.

Salamanders are confusing in their nomenclature because many look alike in general appearance and yet many of the same species are very different. They are generally brightly colored, many-spotted, and have beautiful eyes with black pupils. Their feet and legs are perhaps their most intriguing feature: the front feet have four toes each and the hind legs have five toes. Salamanders are delicate in appearance but

Togetherness is what it's all about and these western newts live a long time in a vivarium.

If you need a lesson in swimming watch the marbled newt for a while.

can run quite fast. The salamander uses his tail for locomotion and balance.

Salamanders delight in a diet of worms and small plant insects, which they relish. They are like chameleons in that, when stalking prey, they sneak up on prospective food in a catlike manner.

You can use a shallow terrarium for these pets, and a bog or woodland situation is what they want. Put in plants like marsh marigolds, and have a large rock protruding from the water. Dry-land area is absolutely necessary so your salamander won't drown if he passes into the air-breathing stage while in your terrarium. Put mosses and ferns in his home, and have a 2-inch gravel base.

Salamanders you may find at pet shops or in your local area include:

Japanese newt (*Molge pyrrhogastra*). Frequently sold in pet shops; 4 inches long, hardy, and takes food easily.

Long-toed salamander (*Ambystoma macrodactylum*). Grows to 5 inches. Endangered species, so do not buy or collect.

Marbled salamander (*A. opacum*). Grows to 4 inches and rarely enters water. Will be at home in a woodland vivarium where there is a dish of water.

Mole salamander (*A. talpoideum*). Four inches long and likes a somewhat wet environment.

Purple salamander (*Gryinophilus porphyriticus*). Should be avoided — he burrows and creates havoc with plants.

Red salamander (*Pseudotriton ruber*). Spends its time in land and water; grows to 6 inches and makes a good pet.

Red-backed salamander (*Plethoden cinerus*). Of medium size and does well in the wooded garden. Lives on land. A good pet.

Red-spotted newt (*Triturus viridescens*). A fair pet and generally available in pet stores.

Tiger salamander (*Ambystoma tigrinum*). A fair pet, but hides and is difficult to find.

Western newt (*Taricha*). Mainly a land dweller but enters water at breeding time. Rough-skinned and cute; excellent pet.

Zigzag salamander (*Plethodon dorsalis*), ravine salamander (*P. richmondi*), and wellers salamander (*P. welleri*) are others you may encounter.

Geckos

Here is a charming group of lizards from Africa, Madagascar, and Australia, but they range worldwide too, with one species, the banded gecko, from the United States. These are perky little animals, useful destroyers of insects, and utterly fascinating pets. They are secretive though and prefer nighttime to day browsing. The gecko can, with its amazing feet, dance across a floor with amazing speed or even clamber up a wall and ceiling with little trouble.

Like all lizards, geckos shed their skins periodically: the old dead skin splits down the back, resembling tissue paper. Geckos also have very fragile tails, so don't pick them up by this appendage or it may come loose. His tail is the gecko's escape mechanism, and if it is grasped by a predator he simply leaves it behind and grows a new one. Another interesting characteristic of geckos is their eyes; most geckos have no movable eyelids. The pupils are vertical in shape, like a cat's.

Like chameleons, some geckos can change color, although the body markings remain the same (the hue changes). When the emerald gecko of Madagascar is disturbed, its green color turns blue-green and somewhat brown.

Geckos depend on their environment for their body tem-

Leopard geckos make good pets once they become accustomed to their new conditions.

The Madagascan day gecko is a capable acrobat scaling walls, ceilings, with ease. Keep him well confined or he will wander. An excellent pet, however.

perature, so suitable levels are 75° to 90°F. In lesser temperatures they will not be active. They are extremely sensitive to cold, and in extreme warmth they may die. Unlike some animals, geckos can live in a confined space for a long time, although the cover should always be in place or they may develop wanderlust. If they do escape don't panic; they generally make themselves comfortable in close proximity to the cage.

Most geckos eat small live insects and meal worms without too much prodding. Be sure the worms are small enough for the lizard to swallow with ease in one gulp. As a supplement, feed geckos a mixture of equal parts molasses, honey, and cod liver oil with a few drops of orange juice. Generally geckos eat more food than they need during their active times and store the fat in their tail for leaner times.

In captivity some geckos are always shy and do not like to be handled; they will nip your fingers when you pick them up. Other geckos respond very well to being pets and eventually become quite tame.

A woodland garden suits most geckos, but a few prefer desert habitats. Include a food dish and a water dish in the vivarium and dry and wet areas.

Perhaps the most popular gecko in pet shops is the banded gecko, who comes in a variety of color patterns. He has smooth velvety skin, is quite small, about 5 inches, and after he knows you, you can pick him up (but not by the tail). Cradle him upside down in the palm of your hand. This species feed on insects, is a nonclimber, and can be housed in a tropical or desert scene. The Moorish gecko is another favorite, only 5 inches long, handsome, and alert and eventually will become a gentle pet; but the round-toed gecko, which is rarely more than an inch long, never becomes used to a vivarium.

Tokay geckos (*Gekko gecko*) are at most pet shops, but they are apt not to be too happy in captivity and can, if

A conglomerate of pastel colors, the frog-eyed gecko is really a charming creature.

Though it is daytime the fat-tailed gecko sleeps away the hours to awaken in the evening, but he is so beautifully colored in browns and blacks he is well worth having.

provoked, produce a rather painful bite. They are quite large, about 12 inches, and are really not too suitable for the home terrarium but satisfactory for the advanced hobbyist. The Indian fat-tailed gecko is docile, can live happily for years in a confined area, and can become a treasured pet. He is yellow or cream with darker markings and his tail is swollen. He is expensive and seldom available in pet shops. The Madagascan day gecko is vividly colored, a fine green with a blue-tinted tail. Unlike most geckos, he is active by day and most alert. This is both good and bad for he will make a dash for freedom at the slightest opportunity.

As mentioned, the species of gecko you get depends on the pet shop you frequent. Some import many animals, while others may only have the banded geckos. Ideal geckos for the vivarium include:

Ashy gecko (*Sphaerodactylus cinereus*). Nocturnal, 2 inches long, and likes warmth. Woodland environment is satisfactory.

Ground banded gecko (*Coleonyx variegatus*). Western lizard about 5 inches long; likes a sandy rocky habitat, and makes an excellent pet. Tames quickly and never bites.

Leaf-toed gecko (*Sphaerodactylus xantii*). A small charmer that lives in rocks and stone crevices.

Leopard gecko (*Eublephorous macularis*). Gentle and beautiful; sometimes called fat-tail gecko.

Madagascan day gecko (*Phelsuma lineata*). Vividly colored and active by day. Difficult to find, but worth the search.

Mediterranean gecko (Hemidactylus). Five inches long, he is at home in a woodland habitat, and don't be frightened if you hear a mouselike squeak from him.

Moorish gecko (*Tarentola mauretanica*). A frequent pet of European children. It grows to 4 inches and occasionally can be found in pet shops in the United States.

Reef gecko (*Sphaerodactylus notatus*). Only 2 inches. Generally nocturnal and lives in a woodland environment; likes warmth.

Round-toed gecko (*S. elegans*). Only 1 inch long, shy, and difficult to keep in captivity.

Tokay gecko (*Gekko gecko*). Handsome, but generally too large (to 14 inches) for home vivariums; furthermore, they bite.

Other geckos from this large group include: Fat-tail gecko, Fringed gecko, Frog-eyed gecko, Malayan house gecko (Hemidactylus), and Monarch's gecko.

Lizards

These are favorite pets, with brilliant and beautiful colors, but many are needlessly killed once they are in a terrarium. Actually, they need more care and attention than easy-to-keep turtles or salamanders. But if their requirements are known, they can become quite docile.

Iguanid lizards are the ones most often seen in shops. These are desert reptiles, although they are also found in nondesert habitats. In their terrarium be sure to include stones or rocks on which they can bask in the sun; this is a must. Once the animal reaches its body-activity temperature (this varies from group to group) it becomes active. Iguanas are not above eating plants, so be prepared. Like most lizards, these animals have fragile tails, and although they may appear sluggish they can move quite fast. Small insects and ants are fare for most lizards.

Iguana, top; horned toad

There are many different kinds of lizards, but here are some you might find at pet shops (or collect yourself):

Californian horned lizard (*Phrynosoma coronatum frontale*). The most common lizard sold in shops. Makes a fine pet. Prefers flat sandy terrain with low vegetation; desert vivarium is fine.

Caimans are sold in pet shops as baby "alligators." They need warmth (90°F) and a land and water situation. They have a selective diet and will bite you every chance they get. Because they can grow quite large, and no one wants an alligator in the bathtub, forget this one. There are too many other more suitable animals for small gardens. (Caimans are crocodiles, not lizards, but for simplicity are included here.)

Chameleon (*Anolis carolinensis*). A favorite pet; always interesting and produces hours of fascinating viewing. Grows to 6 inches. Best in a tropical habitat. Also see page 51.

Common basilisk (*Basilisk americanus*). Often at pet shops, but is too large to keep at home; reaches 24 inches. Also, they are aggressive lizards and never friendly in any situation.

Desert horned toad (*Phrynosoma platyrhinos*). The popular horned lizard. Must be kept warm. Delights in burying himself in sand; needs a desert terrain. Generally amenable; feed him ants to keep him healthy. Grows to 4 inches.

Eastern collared lizard (*Crotaphytus collaris collaris*). An aggressive but handsome lizard, amazingly adroit at hiding, so he is not a particularly good subject (although sold a lot). Desert or woodland terrarium.

Iguana (*Iguana iguana*). Becoming a popular pet, but if you get one, be prepared. He can grow to 24 inches, so have proper facilities. A notorious plant eater; since I prefer a

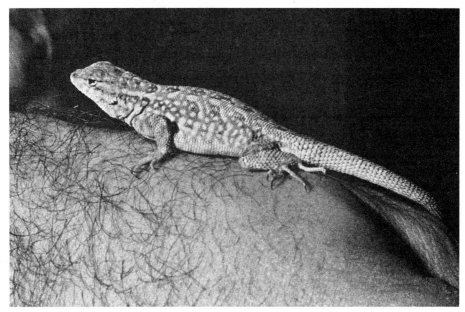

A side-blotched lizard out of his home for a stroll.

Green iguanas are lovely, handsome animals. This one is quite aware we are taking his picture.

Fence lizards are shy at first but eventually become tame. They are burrowers. If you look at the left side of the aquarium you will see one with just his head peeking out.

natural scene of plants and animals, I have never kept one. If you want an iguana, see spiny-tailed iguana, which doesn't eat plants.

Northern chuckwalla (*Sauromalus obesus*). Not a very attractive creature; grows too large (9 inches) and eats plants like candy. Avoid him at all costs although you will find him plentiful in pet shops.

Short or pigmy horned lizard (*Phrynosoma douglassii douglassii*). More tolerant of cold than most lizards and makes a good pet. He is 2 to 3 inches long and needs a sandy arid habitat.

Side blotch uta (*Uta stansburiana stansburiana*). A perky little fellow, curious, and about 4 inches long. He has been a resident of my desert garden for 6 months and is little trouble to care for.

Southern fence lizard (*Sceloporous undulatus*). A great climber and grows to 3 inches. Desert terrarium. A good pet; alert and attractive.

Spiny-tailed iguana (*Ctenosaura pectinita*). Can grow large, but unlike his relative the standard iguana, he eats insects, not plants. A fairly good pet for tropical vivariums.

Western fence lizard (*Sceloporus occidentalis biseriatus*). Likes a desert terrain with some rocks and tree branches. Burrows at night in our vivarium.

Skinks

Skinks have a certain fascination about them. They are curious large-headed, long-tailed creatures, and you will occasionally see them at pet shops. When young, many have blue tails. North American skinks are ground dwellers and are difficult to tell apart.

Skinks are very fast, frighten easily, and do not like to be

This water skink may not look too handsome but close-up he really is an attractive creature. Although he is a water skink, he spends most of his time on land.

handled. Like most lizards, skinks eat worms, grubs, and insect larvae, and will drink water from a dish.

Some you might find are:

Four-striped skink (*Eumeces tetragrammus*). Grows to 3 inches; secretive and not a good pet. Woodland vivarium.

Mountain skink (*E. callicephalus*). Three inches long. Can tolerate some cold.

Short-lined skink (*E. brevilineatus*). Somewhat less shy than a four-striped skink. Woodland vivarium with stone or rock.

Striped red-tailed skink (*E. egregius*). Prefers a woodland terrarium.

Water skink (Lygosoma). Does not seem to be true to his common name for he spends most of his time on land. A pretty fellow and quite alert compared to his shy brothers.

Western skink (*Eumeces skiltonianus*). Lives in a woodsy grassland and needs rocks and logs for cover or he won't be happy at all.

Turtles

Turtles are perhaps the most popular pet sold, but unfortunately thousands of them die once taken from the pet shop. There is no excuse for this, because with adequate care these whimsical fellows live a long time and provide lots of fun. If you give them a natural home — and this is the purpose of this book — they will adapt and eventually become valuable pets.

Remember that turtles carry salmonellosis, a serious disease, so exercise some health measures when handling them. Always wash your hands after playing with turtles, and to avoid any possibility of contamination don't handle your turtle once he is in his new home. This is best for you and the turtle for he doesn't like to be picked up or petted.

The turtles that live only in water are more difficult to keep than those that can live on land with small areas of water nearby. Many turtles cannot swallow their food in the air

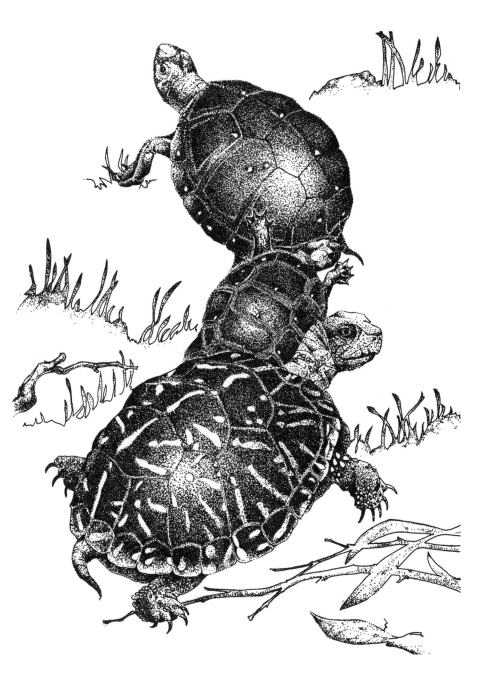

Spotted turtle, top; box turtle

and thus have to eat under water, so you must provide water for them.

Today there are many varieties of turtles available, including foreign species, and some make better pets than others. A few states have strict laws about turtles; your pet dealer will alert you. If in doubt, check with the local fish and game department, listed in the phone book.

Red-eared turtles are frequently at pet stores and make fine pets, never getting too large.

Because there are hundreds of different kinds of turtles we can't list them all, but it isn't necessary anyway; the pet store in your locale will stock suitable species.

A turtle's diet depends on the turtle itself, but most eat small bits of lean beef or raw chicken. (Do not feed turtles cooked meat.) Turtles also eat earthworms, mealworms, and such vegetables as lettuce, carrots, or small pieces of fruit.

A diamond backed terrapin will live for years as a pet. Wash hands after handling any turtle.

Food should be chopped into little pieces that the animal can swallow whole with no trouble. (Exceptions to diet are noted in the following list.)

In the turtle's home, remember to change the water as soon as it gets cloudy.

Water Turtles

Keep in shoreline terrarium: a few inches of water at one end and dry land at the other, with the temperature from 75° to 85°F by day, less at night.

Common mud turtle (*Kinosternon subrubrum*). A not-so-nice guy who is apt to snap at the slightest provocation. Because he is small (to 5 inches), you might want to put up with him since eventually he will become quite tame. Will also adapt to land environment.

Common musk turtle (*Sternotherus odoratus*). Has a mouse-like face, is not very attractive, and smells bad. Avoid him!

Common snapping turtle (*Chelydra serpentina serpentina*). Avoid him. True to his name, he snaps, and the bite can draw blood. Furthermore, he is an aggressive guy that will bully other turtles.

Eastern painted turtle (*Chrysemys picta picta*) and Western painted turtle (*C. p. belli*) are sometimes at pet shops. Small turtles (to 6 inches), and ideal as pets. Treat the same way as the Southern painted turtle.

Mobile turtle (*Pseudemys floridana mobilensis*). Another popular pet, and among the tamest of the water turtles. Eats well, both leafy vegetables and meat, and eventually becomes quite large (to 12 inches), so be prepared.

Northern diamondback terrapin (*Malaclemys terrapin terrapin*). A great charmer and a fun-loving turtle. If you see one for sale, get it. Is robust, lives many years with good care, and rarely grows over 6 inches.

Red-eared turtle (*Pseudemys scripta elegans*). The most popular pet store turtle. He's about the size of a half dollar and quite pretty. Eats in the water. If this little fellow seems nervous when you first get him, don't panic; in a few days he becomes quite settled and tame. He eventually grows to 7 inches.

Sawbuck turtle (*Graptemys pseudogeographica kohnii*). Easy to raise, but always remains quite timid and never likes to be handled. Needs somewhat warmer environment than other turtles, at least 85°F by day.

Southern painted turtle (*Chrysemys picta dorsalis*). Small (only 5 inches when mature), and an inquisitive fellow. He's an attractive dark brown, with a red stripe down his back.

Land/Water Turtles

The following wood and box turtles fall between the water turtles and the true land turtles. Supply a woodland or bog terrarium with an area of water, with moderate heat (75°F) by day. Put plants on upper levels only. These are handsome fellows, adjust easily to their surroundings, and are my favorite turtles. Also, they seem to get along in a confined space if they have to.

Eastern Box turtle (*Terrapene carolina*). Very common and generally spends most of his time on land, although he prefers damp places near water. Makes an excellent pet, and at maturity measures about 6 inches. Woodland habitat is fine.

Spotted turtle (*Clemmys guttata*). Attractive, gentle, loves bog conditions, and rarely strays too far from water. He will take some time before he is actually at home, but once established he is an excellent pet.

Western Box turtle (*Terrapene ornata*). Another fine performer for the somewhat drier garden. Can be housed handsomely in the tropical vivarium, although some water should be provided for him.

Wood turtle (*Clemmys insculpta*). Alert, active, and needs some space to roam. An excellent pet that prefers dry land to water, but possession is illegal in some parts of the United States. Woodland garden.

Hermann's tortoise is a robust turtle that lives for years as a pet.

Land Turtles

These are charming creatures that adapt well to vivarium living. They are robust and with minimum care can live for many years. A desert or tropical habitat suits them:

Gopher tortoise (*Gopherus polyphemus*). A delightful pet and strictly a land animal. He's gentle and interesting; give him plenty of space.

Greek tortoise (*Testudo graeca*). Prefers desert or dry woodlands.

Red-footed tortoise (*Geochelone carbonaria*). Native to South America. Likes warmth and humidity; give him a tropical scene. However, be sure he gets some water to drink. A really attractive turtle and does very well in a vivarium.

Snakes

Snakes come in many sizes and colors. And what fascinating colors! Bright greens and brilliant reds, a kaleidoscope of color than makes them a spectacle in themselves. There are also poisonous snakes such as copperheads and rattlesnakes (certainly not for the home vivarium); while poisonous snakes are few compared to the many snakes known, the idea keeps me from really becoming a snake man. The few snakes I dealt with for this book either were viewed at the Steinhart Aquarium in San Francisco or were offerings from neophyte explorers in my neighborhood. Perhaps as age overtakes me, my courage will return and snakes will intrigue me more.

In the meantime I feel it appropriate to include a few snakes here for basically many of them are good pets and provide endless hours of fascinating viewing. Also, by observing snakes firsthand many people may lose their aversion for them.

Because the youngsters that gave me the snakes were small, so were their pets and just as well. However, the snakes were not mature and they can grow 3 to 4 feet long so be forewarned.

While boas and constrictors are popular now, and indeed a friend I know keeps a lovely boa, we will not be discussing these giants here. By the way, my friend uses his pet boa as a watchdog. Says he leaves it in the reception hall of his home when he is away and no culprit has dared enter (the hall is visible through side glass windows). He further assures me that Cora (the boa) is gentle, lovable, and a perfect pet. And quieter than a dog!

Pacific gopher snakes seem to live with ease in a glass garden. However, when mature they can reach four feet, so be prepared.

Snakes are found in wooded, desert, tropical, or bog habitats. In short, in many environments in the temperate and tropical world. However, in general, most snakes are housed in a woodland or desert vivarium. They will need a dish of water and food at least once a week, although this depends on their size.

The California king snake comes striped or banded; he seems docile enough behind the glass of a vivarium but must be kept by himself. If too hungry he will feast on other snakes. The Pacific gopher snake can live in a confined area

The California king snake is incredibly alert and responds to a tap on the glass.

for some time and will be at home in a woodland scene. The corn snake and yellow rat snake are other colorful pets although the rat snake may at times try to nip you, but only if he is provoked.

Garter snakes are found in many states and I remember them from childhood. These creatures usually tame easily and if you put them in a woodland garden be sure there are rocks or sticks they can hide under. A further advantage of having a garter snake is that it will eat dead food such as pieces of fish if you are squeamish about feeding pets live food.

The other snakes mentioned need a diet of small mice, lizards, or frogs.

5. The Gardens

Setting the scene for your animal friends is part of the fun of living gardens. There is immense satisfaction in creating a greenery that sustains itself with little trouble and at the same time is pleasing to view. Nature is full of tricks, and only in the lilliputian garden can you see them performed. And as mentioned, plants grow luxuriantly in a protected environment, and most animals thrive with plants.

However, don't think that all will be beauty without some attention from you. As with your home, grooming and cleaning are necessary. The inhabitants of the garden — lizards, frogs, chameleons — scamper, prance, and dance about enjoying the environment and at times upset plants or occasionally put things in disarray.

No matter which world you imitate — desert, woodland, tropical, or bog — you will have hours of fascinating viewing and a dividend to boot, for most greeneries make handsome decorative accessories.

The Desert Terrarium

This is perhaps the easiest habitat to assemble and maintain. Desert plants through the ages have learned to take care of themselves, and once planted they need little attention. The main point to remember is that plants need soil around

A fence lizard suns himself on a rock in the garden. Miniature succulents and cacti are all part of the scene.

their roots. If you put them directly into sand, growth will be sparse, if at all. Set up planting islands with open areas with a sand base for animals (sand should be fine-grained). Put in a 5-inch bed, enough so animals can bury themselves; horned lizards in particular delight in burrowing.

Place a few rocks in the vivarium, but prop them so animals can, if they want, get out of the heat and into the shade. (The rocks hold the heat of the day to warm the animals at night.) Water is necessary but should be isolated in a dish or similar container. The dish should be large enough to allow animals to get wet all over; this helps them shed their old skins. Do not be concerned if animals don't drink water from the dish, since they are more prone to take moisture from droplets on plants or rocks. Thus, mist vegetation and stones occasionally.

Depending on the size of the terrarium, an ordinary light bulb (20 to 40 watts) in a reflector shade (aquarium style) will supply sufficient heat. The bulb should be 6 to 12 inches above the surface of the garden. In our 12×12×20 terrarium we use a 20-watt bulb. It is used mainly in the winter for about six hours a day, in the summer and spring perhaps an hour a day. You must judge the heat from observing your animals and how they react to the warmth: Do they cluster under it or avoid it?

Whether you leave the top of the terrarium open or not depends on the animals. Turtles and horned lizards cannot escape if sides are smooth and high. If you deem a cover necessary, use wire screen, not glass, since temperature buildup and humidity can have adverse effects on plants and animals.

There are hundreds of miniature succulents and cacti for the desert scene, and because there are so many, pick and choose. Some, like *Gymnocalycium mihanovichii* (chin cactus), are desirable because of their lovely colors, as are haworthias and kalanchoes. Some, such as rebutias, which are only 2 to 3 inches high, bloom in the terrarium if given enough sun. Echeverias, highly colored plants, look like they are carved from stone; you might want a few, although animals will mar their jadelike finish. Lobivias and parodias are festooned with colorful flowers at bloom time and are always welcome. The powder-puff cactus (*Mammillaria bocasana*) and the old-lady cactus (*M. hahniana*), interesting curiosities in themselves, are right at home in the desert scene, as are the diminutive tigers jaws (Faucaria) and splendid inchworm plant (*Kleinia pendula*).

Put plants in pleasing groups in rear corners of the terrarium. Remember to utilize the decorative leaf markings and varied textures of cacti and succulents as you assemble the picture. Don't worry about spines on cactus hurting creatures;

A side-blotched uta and a fence lizard come up to take a closer look at the photographer.

desert animals have been living with them for ages. Leafy plants like philodendrons or marantas will not survive long, so don't waste your time with them. As mentioned, the floor of the desert garden must be sand; use a 5-inch sand base, except where plants are to be placed. Fill these holes with a porous soil, and then scatter sand over the soil.

Remember that baby iguanas or some of the tortoises may eat plants. If they do, suspend plants in pots from wires at the top of the terrarium; the effect will be a unique floating garden.

This tiny red-footed tortoise is not too happy in his desert home. Later I put him in a tropical environment where he was much more receptive and alert.

Do not neglect watering plants. In the desert they may survive for months without water, but in the terrarium they can't. I water the desert greenery three times a week in spring and summer, twice a week during the rest of the year. Be sure some sunlight reaches the terrarium so plants can live.

Warmth is essential in the desert vivarium. Keep temperatures at least 90°F during the day and at night 10° to 15°F lower.

The following plants are a mere sampling of the many kinds available:

DESERT PLANTS

Adromischus clavifolius. Small, with club-shaped leaves flecked with reddish marks.

A. maculatus (calico hearts). Thick gray-green flat leaves spotted with brown; can bloom in terrariums. Flowers are tipped red-white.

Aeonium atropurpureum. Grows somewhat large (to 18 inches), but stays small in terrarium. Exquisite dark maroon leaves that resemble cabbage roses. Good contrast for animals, and stout stems make for great climbing.

Aloe brevifolia variegata. Rarely grows over 5 inches in diameter; beautiful vertically striped leaves laced with lines of white.

Astrophytum myriostigma (bishop's hood). This old favorite is a spineless odd plant shaped like a bishop's hood.

Cephalocereus senilis (old man cactus). An elongated barrel best describes this plant that is covered with white woolly hairs. It grows slowly. An oddity, but good for terrariums because it is able to withstand abuse by animals.

Crassula arboresenes (silver dollar). Large silvery leaves with red margins and dots.

C. schmidtii. A charming dwarf plant with pink leaves.

Euphorbia obesa (basketball plant). Grows to about 5 inches in diameter. A real curiosity: perfectly round gray-green ball with purple seams. Grow one if there is space in the container; animals cannot harm them in any way.

Faucaria tigrina (tiger's jaw). An attractive gray-green plant spotted white; sometimes bears yellow flowers indoors.

Gasteria liliputana. Thick stubby dark green leaves in a spiral pattern, mottled pale green. Indestructible.

Gymnocalycium mihanovichii (chin castus). Attractive and brightly colored; green with a red crown.

Haworthia fasciata (zebra haworthia). This small plant has dark green leaves banded crosswise with rows of white dots.

Kleinia mandraliscae. Another fine species in this overlooked genus, with gray-green stems and finger-shaped leaves.

K. reptans (blue chalk sticks). This indeed does look like its common name: blue-green cylindrical leaves in clusters. A remarkable plant and great for vivariums; lizards perched on top look like prehistoric monsters.

Mammillaria bocasana (powder-puff cactus). This globular bizarre beauty is a mound of soft fluffy white hairs; surprises occasionally by bearing creamy flowers. Kids love it.

Rebutia kupperiana. This small gray globe will produce myriads of red blooms in the vivarium. Only 2 inches across; a must.

R. minuscula (crown cactus). A lilliputian plant only a few inches around with vibrant red blooms.

Sedum stahlii (Boston beans). Tiny leaves only half an inch long.

Sempervivum arachnoideum (cobweb houseleek). Gray-green rosettes of hairy leaves laces with silver webs. Attractive, but sometimes gets untidy in a vivarium.

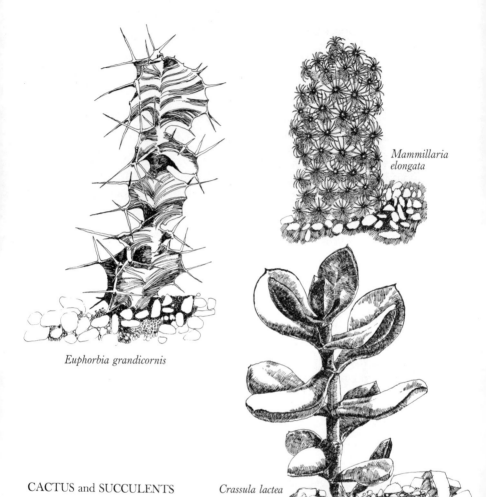

Mammillaria elongata

Euphorbia grandicornis

CACTUS and SUCCULENTS

Crassula lactea

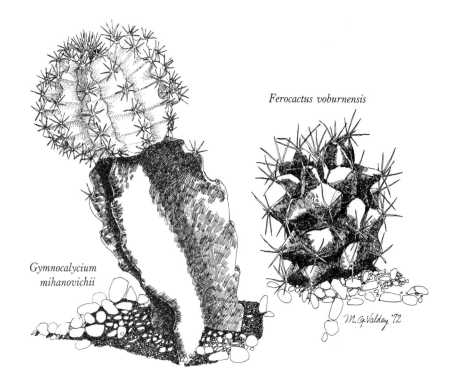

Ferocactus voburnensis

Gymnocalycium mihanovichii

M. G. Valdez '72

The Tropical Garden

Similar to the woodland garden (which is described in the next section), the tropical habitat is arranged in the same way but with different plants. This is the place to use many miniature species of the plant world, and more delightful plants are hard to find. Colorful African violets, tapestry-veined begonias, and exquisite marantas are all part of this world and thrive, where otherwise they might die on a windowsill. Tuck a wee orchid into a corner; add pteris ferns and small house plants, but do not add creepers or vines that will engulf the garden. These tropical plants may give you a jungle, so keep grooming and cutting to always have room for fresh green growth. Don't forget mosses and lycopodiums, always a delight.

Plan a canyon with deep crevices that can be planted with minute ferns such as *Camptosorus rhizophyllum* (walking fern). For accent use a group of rocks etched with emerald moss. Other possibilities are miniature shrubs, trees, or house plants like peperonias and African violets. Use a rich house-plant soil for this garden over a 3-inch bed of gravel topped with charcoal chips.

The tropical terrarium is warm, 75° to 85°F by day and about 65°F at night. If natural bright light is not available for plants, use a 20-watt bulb in an ordinary aquarium reflector. Cover with a screen if you use artificial light or too much heat will accumulate inside; otherwise a glass cover is fine.

The tropical garden is home for chameleons, special frogs, and many geckos; give them protection from the sun with stone ledges or slate embankments. If you cannot locate ferns or mosses, include ground covers like baby's tears, Irish moss, and so forth, which are all available at most nurseries.

In a tropical garden a chamelon is right at home. Remember, you must sprinkle foliage with water for him and provide live insects for food. Meal worms we tried in the bottle cap at left were not touched.

Angraecum compactum. A charming diminutive orchid with large white flowers. Plant in pockets of osmunda fiber.

Anthurium scherzianum. A popular house plant that grows to 12 inches, with bright red spathe. Loves the conditions of the tropical terrarium.

Ascocentrum miniatum. Orange flowers crown this 5-inch orchid; has a bright color and is so dependable.

Bulbophyllum barbigerum. An intricate orchid with purple-brown hairs; loves warmth and sun. *B. morphologorum* is another good candidate, with hundreds of minute yellow-brown flowers that form a crown.

Caladium humboldti 'Little Rascal'. Fine foliage accent with lance-shaped, wine-red foliage.

Calathea picturatum argentea. Another good accent plant, with silver leaves etched in dark green.

Camptosorus rhyzophyllus. A diminutive charmer, with spade-shaped evergreen fronds.

Chamaeranthemum igneum. A tropical creeper with velvety bronze-brown leaves and pink veins.

Cirrhopetalum cumingii. A stunning orchid; only 2 inches high, with red and pink flowers in a half-circle design.

Cryptanthus bromeliodes tricolor. A fine bromeliad; small with rosettes of green leaves striped pink and white.

Episcia. Spreading plants with velvety leaves in exquisite colors and a bonus of charming flowers. Select from the many small species that are available.

Ficus radicans variegata. A creeper, with silver-green leaves marked white; *F. pumila* is also interesting with its heart-shaped leaves and disks that cling to glass.

Hedera helix (English ivy). A tempting plant with bright ivy-shaped leaves, but invariably it expires in a terrarium. Still, the challenge is worth a try.

Helxine soleirolii (baby's tears). A charming bright green ground cover for shady areas.

Humata tyermannii. Small and delicate with lacy fronds.

Microlepia setosa. A delicate fern with feathery fronds.

Philodendron. Many of these popular plants can be grown in a tropical garden. Select small-leaved kinds (there are too many to mention). Plant in pockets of osmunda fiber.

Polystichum setiferum (hedge fern). This fine fern has feathery fronds covered with brown hairlike scales.

Pothos (Scindapsus) aureus. A climber, with ovate green leaves blotched with yellow; grows fast and will need pruning. Plant in pockets of osmunda fiber.

Pteris cretica (ribbon fern). A charmer, with delicate fronds to 6 inches.

Restrepia elegans. A 2-inch lovely orchid that produces a fantastic yellow flower dotted red; must be seen to be believed. Plant in pockets of osmunda fiber.

Saxifraga sarmentosa (strawberry geranium). Neither a strawberry nor a geranium, but always a favorite, with its round and hairy silver-veined leaves. Plant in pockets of osmunda fiber.

Don't forget miniature begonias, geraniums, and African violets for the woodland garden. There is an infinite array of these delightful charmers, too many to list here, but there are fine books you might want to consult (see Appendix).

MOSSES. Mosses are the finishing touch to small gardens, and the following ones have proved satisfactory for us: Climacium, Mnium, Rhodobryum, Grimmia, and Rhagcomitrium.

Humata tyermannii

Polystichum tsus simense   FERNS

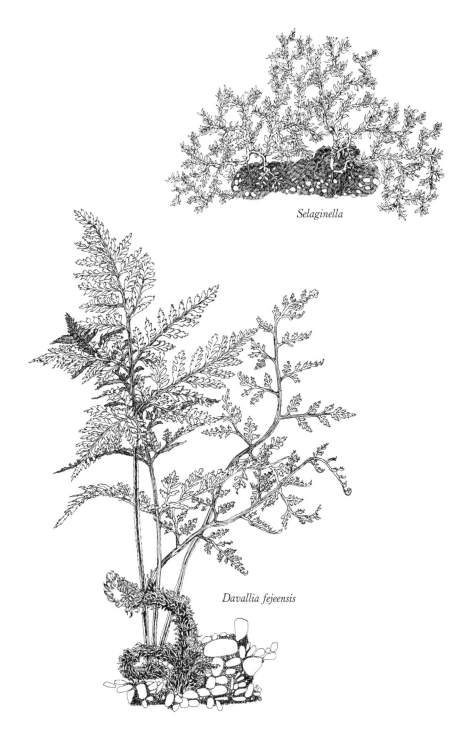

Selaginella

Davallia fejeensis

Peperomia caperata

Philodendron sodiroi

HOUSE PLANTS

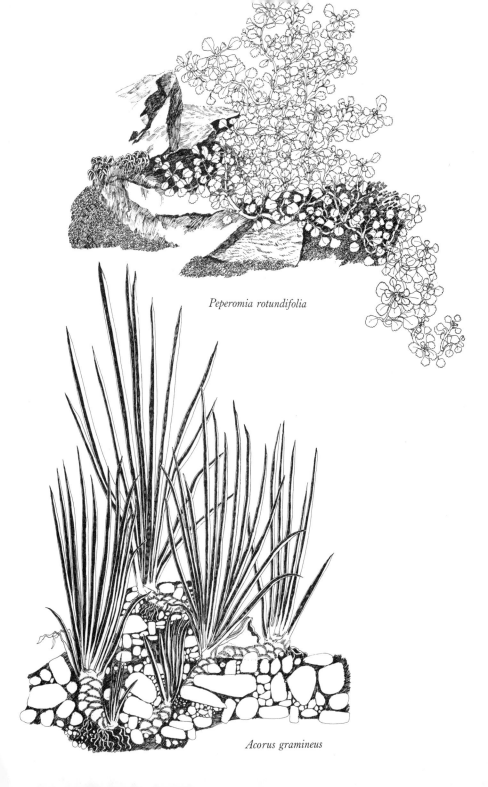

Peperomia rotundifolia

Acorus gramineus

The Woodland Garden

This little piece of nature has always been one of my favorites because it combines lovely forest denizens like hepatica and wintergreen with some charming frogs and lizards. The environment should be somewhat cool and moderately moist with good humidity. The jewels of the forest — mosses, ferns, and lichens — should be tucked into crannies and nooks to make delightful surprises fresh with dew and glistening like silver in early morning light.

Think of nature's woodland scenes — a New England forest floor perhaps. The habitat is cool, humid, and somewhat damp, where native plants such as partridge berry (Mitchella) and bloodroot (Sanguinaria) thrive. Wild orchids and violets glisten in morning light and emerald green mosses festoon the scene.

Although the desert garden is sparsely planted, woodlands abound with plants. Don't forget to put in some interesting stones and perhaps a twig to simulate a tree branch. And don't forget low rock ledges, which animals love. In the center of the landscape have open space for the creatures (this allows you to see them clearly). Use hills and valleys to create a miniature terrain, place plants where they are in scale to each other, and utilize leaf textures and color. Use bright green species with dark green foliage; strive for contrast and drama.

Temperature in the woodland garden should be about 60°F at night and 65 to 75°F during the day. This garden will be ecologically balanced, for the amphibians will absorb moisture from the soil and the reptiles will not bake, for this is a garden with very little sun but with ample light. Furthermore, a glass top will keep moisture in and humidity high. Place the glass on tiny wood blocks on top of the case so some air can circulate in the greenery.

A woodland garden made a perfect home for the author's pet geckos. One is a fringed gecko. The other is a Malayan house gecko, whom you have to look closely for. He clutches the rock in the center.

Planting plan for the woodland garden can be hill and dale or forest and pond, or for a unique effect use deciduous plants for forcing, such as wee violets and wild pansies. Native plants are fine possibilities too; however, remember that collecting them is prohibited in most states, but native plants are obtainable from suppliers and, in fact, are better than collected specimens (see Chapter 7).

To make the vivarium, cover the bottom with a layer of small pebbles to a depth of three-fourths of an inch. This will serve as a drain for excess water, so plant roots will not be immersed in excessive moisture. Over the pebbles put a 3-inch bed of rich, moderately acid-type fertile soil. Put plants in place, and dampen (do not soak) soil. Keep the garden in a cool, bright place out of sun. Water the plants about once every ten days or when soil feels dry to the touch.

In this garden concentrate on low-growing, ground-hugging plants like mosses and ferns, with only an occasional tall plant. Select plants that are robust and with stout stems because animals will scamper over them.

Terrestrial newts, some fence lizards, frogs, and wood and box turtles are all at home in this environment (see Chapter 4). Small perky tree frogs are fine too, but do not use chameleons or aquatic turtles; it will be too cool for them.

No artificial light is needed for this vivarium.

Woodland Plants

Native plants are rarely amenable in cultivation, but in terrariums they certainly have a better chance of survival than if they were on windowsills. This applies also to lichens and club mosses, which cannot survive as house plants. Certain house plants also supplement the scene; these have outstanding foliage and one (Episcia) offers a bounty of colorful flowers. The following selection is a potpourri, but purposely so:

Acorus gramineus pusillus. This is a compact grassy plant, excellent for corners. Lends good vertical accent; grows to 4 inches.

Adiantum bellum (Bermuda maidenhair). A 6-inch miniature version of the maidenhair fern.

A. hispidulum. Lovely, with dark green branching fronds.

Anoechtochilus roxburghi. A shade-loving exquisitely leaved orchid grown for its velvety green leaves with gold veins.

Arisaema triphyllum (Jack-in-the-pulpit). This native plant needs little introduction: it is a charmer with green striped spathes flushed with purple. Deciduous, difficult to grow, but will succeed in a large terrarium that is very airy and cool.

Calathea argyraea. Low and compact with blotched green leaves laced with silver.

Cypripedium. This is a fantastic group of orchids, and their beauty has made them so much the target of every collector that few native stands remain. I would never suggest any for ordinary windowsill culture (although they are sold for such purposes) nor have I ever recommended them in my orchid books. However, for terrarium growing there are a few that will succeed, but very few. Do not pick them from the forest. Order from local dealers, and get plants into the terrarium immediately; even a day without attention will kill them.

C. acaule (pink lady-slipper). Pink and lovely, but it needs a strongly acid soil.

C. parviflorum. This is the orchid you should try because it will succeed in a cool moist terrarium with slightly acid soil. It bears a fragrant yellow flower atop a 12-inch stem (often confused with *C. pubescens,* which is a larger plant that grows to 24 inches).

C. reginae (showy lady-slipper). A regal orchid that grows to 18 inches, with showy pink blooms. Difficult to grow but not impossible and wants a shady, moist place with slightly acid soil.

Cyrtomium falcatum (holly fern). Somewhat large, but so beautiful with scalloped shiny green leaves.

Dicentra canadensis (squirrel corn). Small, to 10 inches, with fine white flowers; goes dormant soon after flowering, but worth a try.

Striped Pipsissawa

Northern Pitcher Plant

Gold Thread

Trailing Arbutus

WOODLAND PLANTS

Episcia. Fine velvety-leaved plants that bear myriads of colorful flowers. Supposedly prefers warmth, but does quite well in the woodland conditions. Many varieties are available.

Fittonia verschaffeltii (mosaic plant). A fine terrarium subject, with velvety green leaves laced with veins of contrasting color.

Gaultheria procumbens (wintergreen). A good evergreen cover that likes moderately acid soil and shade; white flowers and red berries.

Hepatica acutiloba (sharp-leaved liverleaf). Three-lobed leaves, and flowers may be white or pink. Grows in neutral soil and probably will be the first in the terrarium to bloom.

Lycopodium (club moss). Fine plants to simulate oak, maple, and beech trees; lacy and lush green. Thy these:

L. clavatun (running pine). Long fuzzy stems.

L. complanatum (ground cedar). Trailing stems with fanlike branches to 5 inches long.

L. lucidulum (shining club moss). Has shining scalelike leaves. Barely grows more than an inch a year, so is perfect for vivariums.

L. obscurum (ground pine). Looks like a pine. Branches grow to 10 inches, with spikes sessile.

Maranta massangeana (prayer plant). A kaleidoscope of color: leaves are purple and green. Outstanding.

M. (Ctenanthe) oppenheimiana. Another exotic beauty with multicolored foliage.

Mitchella repens (partridge berry). An evergreen creeper that bears red berries at Christmas and lasts for many weeks.

Spreads easily and needs a moderately acid soil; never let it dry out.

Pellaea rotundifolia (button fern). A decorative plant with dark stems and round green leaves.

Polystichum tsus-simense. Dwarf-growing fern with delicate lacy fronds.

Pteris ensiformis 'Victoriae'. A silver-leafed fern margined with dark green. Many varieties.

Sanguinaria canadensis (bloodroot). A gray-green plant that likes shade. Has white, early spring flowers.

Selaginella. Often called moss ferns, they are neither moss nor fern but soft club mosses:

S. caulescens. Tall, deep green, and lacy, with upright fronds spinning from center.

S. denticulata. Listed so you will avoid it. Has widely separated scales, is bright green, and grows rampant.

S. emmeliana. The one is frequently offered by nurseries; light green in color and lacy.

S. uncinata. Blue-green leaves, grows in bunches; fine terrarium plant.

Sinningia pusilla (miniature gloxinia). A true gem, with soft round leaves and pale lavender flowers. Likes a little more warmth than offered in woodland conditions, but it is worth a try anyway.

TRILLIUMS. A favorite group of many plants, and what you choose depends on conditions in the vivarium. *T. grandi-florum* bears lovely white flowers with pink hues and grows to 18 inches. It needs a moderately acid soil. *T. undulatum* must have very acid soil, so don't try it unless conditions are just right. It has white flowers with a rosy throat. Tubers of trilliums are usually available at suppliers in the fall; plant them at least 2 inches deep in the vivarium.

MOSSES. This is a varied group of fascinating wee plants that are delightful nature studies. There are so many different mosses that they would require a book of their own to due them credit. Here are a few I have tried in vivariums: Rhodobryum, Mnium, Climacium, Bryum, and Timmia.

SMALL TREES. Almost any seedling forest tree can be used in the woodland garden to supply vertical accent. Try some of these: Yew, Hemlock, and White cedar.

The Bog Garden

The bog garden is a magic wonderland where many animals you never can see in the forest or woods go about their daily business of living. The environment is somewhat between the woodland and shoreline garden with respect to moisture. This is where marsh marigolds, partridge berry, and skunk cabbage abound.

Arrange the habitat so there is a 3-inch bed of rich acid soil (4 to 5 PH) mixed with sphagnum moss over a charcoal-and-gravel base; you want the soil damp but never muddy. In a separate area provide a deep dish with clean fresh water for salamanders and frogs, which drink through their skins, not their mouths. Use a large dish that can easily be removed for cleaning. You might want to include some small water plants like bladderwort or water lettuce if the terrarium is large enough. For ground plants, small evergreen trees are ideal: Twinflower and Mitchella are good here too, and so are unique Pitcher plants and Venus flytraps, which are impossible to grow outside a terrarium but are amenabe inside. If the terrarium is tall (at least 24 inches), pitcher plants may

A bog garden is shared by a frog and a skink.

bloom bearing buds that unfurl into fantastic petals; orchids, the jewels of the bog, will bloom too.

Avoid direct sunlight in the bog garden; this should be a shady, moist place. A cover is a must, not only to keep the creatures inside but to maintain a humid atmosphere; the bog garden must never be dry if plants are to flourish.

All kinds of animals can go into this setting: red efts, salamanders, tree frogs, wood frogs, and tiny skinks (see Chapter 4). Avoid turtles since they consume plants. The bog garden offers an endless cycle of life.

Light should be subdued and temperature moderate. 75° to 80°F in the daytime and 60° to 65°F at night (cooling at night is essential for plants and animals).

BOG PLANTS

Adiantum cuneatum gracillimum. A small fern with delicate lacy fronds.

A. pedatum (American maidenhair). Another good fern, with graceful curved fronds.

Andromeda polifolia. Small leathery leaves and light pink flowers make this a desirable terrarium plant. It is a dwarf plant and stay low-growing; ideal.

Asplenium platyneuron (ebony spleenwort). Feathery fronds and brown-purplish stems make this a delightful fern for the tiny garden.

A. trichomanes (maidenhair spleenwort). A 6-inch fern with thick clustered fronds and 1-inch leaflets on black ribs.

Blechnum spicant (deer fern). This is a large but handsome fern; dark green glossy fronds.

Caltha palustris (marsh marigold). Bright yellow buttercup-type flowers dot this spring beauty. Needs its feet in water to thrive.

Chimaphila maculata (striped pipsissewa). Arrow-shaped leaves with lovely veining.

Coptis trifolia. A dainty bog plant with handsome scalloped leaves.

Cornus canadensis (bunchberry). This small cousin of the dogwood tree makes an excellent ground cover in shade. Grows only a few inches high.

Dionaea muscipula (Venus flytrap). A curious insect-eating plant; small, with bright green claw foliage. An oddity.

These two small frogs sit and contemplate each other in a bog garden.

Drosera rotundifolia. A unique plant that is fascinating to watch; has tiny round leaves with hairy blades that capture insects.

Dryopteris cristata. A lovely blue-green fern.

D. linnaeana (oak fern). Dark green and handsome.

Epigaea repens (trailing arbutus). Bright green leaves and white or pink flowers. Needs a very acid soil to survive.

Goodyera pubescens (rattlesnake plantain). A dainty bog plant with oval green leaves veined white.

Houstonia caerulea (bluets). No guarantee that this one will succeed, but the dainty yellow-eyed blue or white flowers make this a definite challenge.

Kalmia polifolio (bog kalmia). Grows to 20 inches; leaves white underneath, and flowers rose-purple.

Mitchella repens (partridge berry). This is the famous partridge berry, a fine evergreen creeper with pinkish-white flowers and red berries.

Polypodium vulgare. Can grow large, but seedlings are fine for habitat; evergreen fronds to 8 inches.

Potentilla fruiticosa. Good shrub with bright yellow flowers; many varieties. Select dwarf kinds.

Sarracenia purpurea (Northern pitcher plant). Green to dark purple pitchers; one of the bizarre insect-eating plants.

Spiranthes cernua (nodding ladies tresses). A bright little orchid with white flowers on a 12-inch stem. Worth a try.

Also try seedlings of Arborvitae, Spruce, White pine, and Yew. Good bog mosses to use are *Aulacomnium palustre, Climacium dendroides, Polytrichum juniperinum,* and *P. strictum.*

The Shoreline Garden

Many salamanders, green frogs, efts, and various turtles need the habitat of the shoreline garden (crocodiles too live in this type of abode). Although shoreline life is indeed interesting to watch, too often this kind of garden requires endless maintenance, for water must occupy at least half the space, and it is difficult to keep clean. Siphoning off uneaten food and excretions is of course possible but not a thankful chore. Still, for those with perseverance, the shoreline garden can provide hours of fascinating viewing.

There are several ways to arrange this garden, but perhaps the easiest is a barrier of glass set across the bottom and dividing the tank; one side is sand and rock, and the other side is gravel, stone, and a few selected plants. Remember that the shoreline must have a swim area and wet land for animals to be at home.

The temperature should be 75° to 85°F in the daytime. An electric light reflector will help keep pets warm, encourage plants to grow, and reduce water loss caused by evaporation. Use tropical plants (see page 104) in the land area, with water plants like Vallisneria and Sagittaria in the water garden. You need a rather large and watertight container, at least of 15-gallon capacity, for this setting. If you like aquarium fishes such as zebras, platies, and neon tetras, keep them in the water area, thus making a combination aquaterrarium.

6. Care of Animals and Plants

Once you purchase animals they are your responsibility. As with a dog or a cat, you must take care of them and give them food and water. If you do not want to devote some time to the creatures, it is better not to have them; neglect is injustice.

In captivity, animals become dependent on you, and even if released later they may not be able to fend for themselves. Proper care includes keeping the vivarium clean and, as mentioned, having live food for the pets; you might want to breed your own meal worms (beetle larvae), or buy them and other foods at pet shops.

Animals: Feeding and Food

Quite frankly, a good deal of success with vivarium animals depends on whether the animal will accept food. Many times in new surroundings they become frightened, confused, and simply refuse to eat. Coaxing them does little good, but persistance pays off. Take out old food and put in new food daily until they start to feed, but do not bother the creatures unduly.

Meal worms are excellent food for many terrarium inhabitants; commercially these worms are raised on bran meal. Grubs and perhaps fruit flies can be obtained from local pet shops. All you need to raise your own meal worms is a metal box; your supplier can help you with initial cultures. Place the box in a dark spot, and be sure it has air holes. Put in a carrot or potato to supply moisture, but otherwise see that no water enters the box or the colony will be ruined.

Many lizards also feed on small grasshoppers, crickets (which are sold at bait shops), houseflies, mosquitoes, and even small bees (caterpillars are also fine fare). All these insects are free for the catching. Plant lice and mites are delectable to many animals, so if your house plants are invaded by insects put your pets to work.

Don't be too concerned if some animals won't accept food for several days; many can, and frequently do, go two weeks without food. If you pet retains his color and is active, the starvation diet is not harming him, so don't try to force him to eat; it won't work.

Small pieces of fruit, and lettuce leaves, are supposedly fine food for some lizards, but ours (the iguana and collared lizards) would never feed on them. Only if it moved would our pets bother with it. Occasionally a lizard approached dead insects but frogs absolutely avoided them.

Sometimes if you run out of food you might try a bit of ground beef on the end of a fine thread. Move it around in front of the animal and see if he responds. I had one chameleon that was especially fond of this diet and would run to the beef whenever I put it in the cage.

The time of day you feed animals makes a difference too; most are active during the day, except most geckos, which are alert at night. Generally, I feed my pets in the morning. If they don't respond I then try afternoon or early evening. In other words, I keep tempting them at different times of the day until I find the right time and then I stick to that. By the way, I found late afternoon the best feeding time for animals.

Freeze-dried foods for turtles and frogs are sold at pet shops, but I so far have had little success with these commercial products. Freeze-dried foods, such as worms, must be soaked in water a few minutes before feeding.

Illness

Small animals are occasionally bothered by illness (colds) or parasites and wounds. Observation is the only way to tell when your animal is sick. Generally, listlessness is a tip-off that something may be awry.

External parasites like black or red mites might attack lizards. They lurk around the folds in the neck, in the crevice between the eyecap and skin, and sometimes in ear openings. Try scrubbing the lizard's skin with a cotton swab dipped in water to eliminate the mites.

Colds or pneumonia are characterized in most lizards by excessive salivation from the mouth and a residue from the nostrils; gasping for breath is another indication. There is little you can do for animals with pneumonia, but sometimes putting them in a warm enclosure with little air circulation but increased humidity helps.

Sometimes lizards have problems shedding their skins. The cage may have high humidity, which makes skins gummy, or a too-dry cage make skins stick to the animals. You can, if you are careful, help lizards by using a long forceps. Try to remove the skin for them without disturbing them too much.

Cuts or abrasions to the nose or mouth, which can occur if lizards rub against wire screens, are best left alone. You can apply an antiseptic, but generally these wounds heal themselves with time.

If eye infections occur, consult your local pet shop; excess fluid accumulates in this condition, and it can be drained off only by an experienced person.

Sometimes an animal simply will not respond to captivity; he won't eat, he sulks, and in general he refuses to live. In this case take him back to the pet shop to see if they will exchange him for another pet. It is better to follow this procedure than to allow the animal to die.

Practical Hints: Animals

Don't crowd vivariums; a few creatures do far better and live far longer than many in the same container.

Use a cover that is foolproof. Tiny tree frogs can squeeze through a crack, and slithery lizards are also masters of escape. A screen cover is generally best, but glass covers are satisfactory too.

Don't try to make your own lighting devices; reflector-type aquarium units are inexpensive and do the job better. Never use fluorescent lamps. Incandescent is necessary because it contains the red light rays that provide heat, which many animals need.

Don't put lighting equipment directly on top of glass covers. They can break if lamps get too hot.

Always provide a natural habitat for the animals; choose scenes as discussed in previous chapters. However, never create complicated settings that discourage cleaning.

Experiment somewhat with different foods for your pets in case meal worms or fruit flies are not available at pet shops.

For all settings, although it is not absolutely necessary, use leakproof containers.

Remove unused food and excreta from vivariums the next day; don't let it accumulate until it smells. (Then it is a nasty job to do.)

Don't handle pets unnecessarily. Many never really get tame, and few really like to be handled.

If a pet does not respond to the captive life or refuses to eat, consult the pet shop or local aquarium.

Do not continually bother animals by tapping on the glass of the vivarium. It startles and frightens them and takes that much longer for them to become acclimated to their new surroundings.

Keep all containers' glass scrupulously clean at all times, but do not use harsh cleansers or window cleaners with ammonia.

Visit your local zoo. By seeing what the professionals do you can get many new ideas of how to display your pets.

Avoid keeping exotic costly creatures until you have had some experience with other animals.

Avoid keeping crocodiles, caymans, etc. They invariably get too large for cases and are not meant for bathtubs. Furthermore, most are protected by law now and should not be sold in pet shops.

If your reptile gets an ailment not covered here, consult local authorities. Call natural history museums and other such public institutions. Although these people are not obliged to give you answers, they invariably are more than happy to help you help your pet.

Practical Hints: Plants

Buy only small plants in 2- or 3-inch pots; large ones are a waste of money and do little good in a terrarium.

Use as many miniatures as possible, but avoid creeping plants and rampant ones that will soon engulf the setting.

Other than native plants, it is rarely necessary to buy by mail. Most florists and nurseries stock small plants for the terrarium.

Do trim frequently overgrown plants; it does little harm to cut them.

When plants get too large for the vivarium, transfer them to pots and grow them on the windowsill. Take babies as they develop (if plants are dividable), and set them back in the terrarium.

Don't ever use insecticides or fertilizers on plants; the

poisonous sprays may kill your pets and since you want plants to stay small, why feed them?

If plants do develop fungus, remove and treat them separately outside the container, and then replace them after a few days. Insects should rarely be troublesome, for frogs and many lizards consume them with relish.

Spray foliage frequently with water on hot summer days but not at all in cold, cloudy weather. (Never spray desert plants.)

Remove all dead leaves, blossoms, and twigs from the container immediately. Don't let debris accumulate.

If certain plants do not respond in the terrarium, remove them and substitute others. There are hundreds to try.

Keep soil for plants moist but never soggy.

7. Collecting Plants and Animals

I do not advocate needless collecting of native plants or animals, but I do think that if an area is being bulldozed, or if you have permission from a property owner, collecting a few specimens should not cause the conservationist any alarm. Actually, it is good, for you are rescuing doomed flora and fauna from certain death. However, collecting on private property is strictly forbidden, as it is in forest preserves and sanctioned garden areas. And, too, many states have laws against collecting native specimens, so check first with local authorities even if permission is given or you are gathering in a prospective building site.

I remember large stands of wild orchids in Wisconsin; on a recent trip the colony was practically nonexistent because of the collecting mania. This is uncalled-for rape of the land and should not be practiced. In fact, if you want wild orchids (and these are delightful plants), do not collect them. Instead, buy nursery plants from specialists; today some of our best wild orchids are being raised by mail-order suppliers.

Collecting Plants

First, before you take the time and trouble to gather your own plants, remember that native plants are difficult to reestablish; they are highly temperamental about soil and conditions. Even the experienced gardener has problems with them, and the novice gardener needs to know a good deal about plants to have them flourish in the vivarium. But in spite of all these drawbacks, plants you gather yourself bring immense satisfaction when grown to peak form. If the challenge seems too much, buy plants from suppliers. From my experience, the supplier's plants are more robust and more apt to succeed in your vivarium than collected specimens.

However, as mentioned, if you can save plants from a bulldozed area do it and save them, not just remove them. When I lived in Illinois my house was on an acre of land that adjoined the forest preserve. Here were nestled hundreds of native plants such as trilliums, wood violets, and so forth. From experience I learned (after much trial and error) the right way to successfully transplant the wild denizens.

A basic requirement (as with many things) is to observe. Just what kind of soil is the plant growing in? Is it in the shade, in sun, in filtered sun? Never take more than one or two plants from a stand of plants; always leave some in the ground. It is senseless rape to take many, for you really need only a few for the vivarium. Don't take plants in full bloom; wait until they are dormant (spring-blooming plants in fall and summer and fall bloomers in early spring). Even though you think that the biggest and largest flowering specimen is the one to remove, invariably it doesn't "work" in the terrarium. Instead, choose a much-less mature plant. Its root system is not fully grown yet, and it has a better chance to survive the move.

Do not yank a plant from the ground. Use a small spade, and mark a deep circle around the plant; remove the plant with a good portion of its native soil. Transplanting is then less of a shock and many times native soil contains a special fungi that plants need to survive.

Once the plants are dug, wrap moist burlap or newspaper

around the roots or use plastic bags stuffed with moist papers.
Keep the collected plants out of the sun, and replant them
as soon as you get home. Have the terrarium ready, and carefully insert plants, filling in with fresh soil; water thoroughly
and keep plants in the shade the first few days. Small ferns,
mosses, wildflowers, and small seedlings of various trees are
all likely candidates for the vivarium.

Identification of plants is last but perhaps should be first.
By all means know what you are collecting. It is senseless just
to pull up everything because it is there, and in many cases
it won't be suitable for your terrarium. Following is a list
of some native plants with descriptions:

Aquilegia canadensis (common American columbine). Grows
about 15 inches, with red-yellow spurred flowers.

Arisaema triphyllum (Jack-in-the-pulpit). These are indeed
getting scarce, so buy rather than collect them. They have
the familiar pulpit-type brownish-green flower.

Caltha palustris (marsh marigold). Light green leaves and
bright marigold-type yellow blooms.

Cornus canadensis (bunchberry). Dogwood-shaped leaves and
white flowers followed by red berries.

Epigaea repens (trailing arbutus). An excellent terrarium
plant; white or pink flowers.

Hepatica acutiloba (hepatica). Flowers usually white or pink
and leaves somewhat maroon in fall.

Mertensia virginica (Virginia bluebells). Fine pinkish-blue
flowers; needs sun or shade.

Mitchella repens (partridge berry). A lovely evergreen with
round, dark green leaves and beautiful red berries.

Polygonatum commutatum (great Solomon's seal). White
flowers and blue fruit; use for shade.

Sanguinaria canadensis (bloodroot). Lobed leaves and white flowers; grows large but is handsome.

Orchids

These are unquestionably the most fascinating wildflowers for the vivarium, but as cautioned, do not collect them in the wild. Treat orchids judiciously for they are difficult plants to establish, but once growing they are indeed a satisfaction.

Cypripedium acaule (pink lady slipper). A lovely shade orchid; succeeds where most orchids might fail.

C. pubescens (yellow lady slipper). Bright yellow flowers; a popular plant.

C. reginae (showy lady slipper). Large (to 14 inches), but bears spectacular rose-white flowers.

Goodyera pubescens (rattlesnake plantain). Grow this one for its handsome evergreen leaves that are veined white.

Ferns

Adiantum pedatum (American maidenhair fern). Graceful, curved, bright green fronds.

Asplenium platyneuron (ebony spleenwort). Grows to 12 inches; feathery fronds with brownish-purple stems.

A. trichomanes (maidenhair spleenwort). Only 6 inches tall but a gem; thick-clustered fronds with 1-inch leaflets on black ribs.

Dryopteris marginalis (marginal shield fern). Many species in this fine group; some large, others small.

Polypodium vulgare (common polypody). Evergreen fronds to about 8 inches; grows easily.

Polystichum acrostichoides (Christmas fern). Evergreen lacy fern; always good in cool vivarium.

Pteris. Delightful wee ferns. They make ideal glass-case plants, including *P. cretica* (ribbon fern), with delicate fronds to about 6 inches, and *P. ensiformis*.

Collecting Animals

Although there is little need to collect your own animals, since pet shops have them in abundance, the idea of observing reptiles in their native haunts is fascinating. It's interesting to see how animals live and then to create your own greenery for them. Within your own state you will find many fascinating reptiles and amphibians — lizards, skinks, frogs — for your vivariums.

For the most part, collecting an animal or two is not harmful, but avoid unwanton gathering of many creatures. Check local fish and game departments to be sure you do not collect endangered species. Furthermore, some animals have "bag" limits: you are only allowed one or two.

Spring is the best time to collect reptiles; the warmth brings them into the open. Fall is the other time. During the summer or winter many reptiles hibernate, except turtles, which are found during summer. Select a warm sunny day for your collecting trip; in overcast or rainy weather few reptiles will be found. Take some sacks (sugar or flour sacks are ideal), and be sure there is string around the top of the bag so it can be tied.

A noosing stick is your main equipment. You can make this from a pole about 5 feet long and a loop of wire or string about 3 inches in diameter left protruding from the end of the pole. Hold the double wire extending the length of the pole in one hand, the pole in the other hand. Place the wire or string noose in back of the reptile's head and then quickly but gently pull tight. For some reason lizards have no fear of the string or wire noose and will approach it without fear, making for an easy capture. Once you snare the animal, release him; handle him at the back of the head and drop him into the sack. Do not put too many specimens into the same sack, and keep them out of direct sunlight; overheating will kill your captures.

To find small animals, overturn flat rocks, pieces of wood, and fallen trees, and then stand aside; once uncovered, lizards move fast, so be ready for them. Inspect crannies and nooks, but warily. *Caution is part of the collector's method.*

You need a long-handled net, similar to a butterfly net, for turtles. Quietly walk the shore of a pond or stream with the net (good results are obtained if you are quiet and cautious).

Reptiles are a fast-disappearing part of nature, and once again I say do not collect them needlessly, or for the sheer fun of catching them. Only if you are going to transfer them to your vivarium is it sensible to capture one or two, but never more.

Amphibian collecting is best after the first fall rains. Use a flashlight to detect the shining eyes of frogs and toads, whose presence may otherwise be overlooked. Or locate frogs by their voices: stop and listen, and then follow in the direction of the animals' sounds. Use a small dip net to catch the amphibians, or grab them in your cupped hand. Handle them gently, and put them immediately into a cloth bag. With amphibians it's a good idea to have damp moss or leaves in the sack, but do not include any soil that can smother the creature. You can also catch frogs and toads near street lights, where they go to find insects. Toads are found near quiet water, in gardens and tall grasses, or any damp place near a house. Walk carefully and quietly when searching for animals. American chameleons, found from North Carolina to Texas, can often be snared as they sleep on leaves at night, or shine a flashlight at them and use a net.

When you capture your lizards or frogs make a mental or written note about the environment so you can intelligently duplicate it in the vivarium. Be prepared for the feeling of the toad or frog in your hand. Remember that the toad is cold and dry; the frog is slippery and wet. Frogs can jump better than toads and are more difficult to catch.

Salamanders and newts hide in wet, moist, and generally muddy places and are difficult to capture or find. They are masters at hiding, so it is better to buy these pets at shops. Also, certain salamanders are on the endangered species list and should not be captured under any circumstances. The ones you buy in shops are those that are not in danger of extinction.

APPENDIX: Common and Scientific Names of Pets Often Found in Vivariums

American chameleon	*Anolis carolinensis*
American toad	*Bufo americanus americanus*
Ashy gecko	*Sphaerodactylus cinereus*
Bullfrog	*Rana catesbeiana*
Californian horned toad	*Phrynosoma coronatum frontale*
Carpenter frog	*Rana virgatipes*
Cayman	Caiman sp.
Common basilisk	*Basilisk americanus*
Common or Eastern mud turtle	*Kinosternon subrubrum*
Common musk turtle	*Sternotherus odoratus*
Common snapping turtle	*Chelydra serpentina serpentina*
Cricket frog	*Acris gryllus gryllus*
Desert horned toad	*Phrynosoma platyrhinos*
Eastern box turtle	*Terrapene carolina carolina*
Eastern collared lizard	*Crotaphytus collaris collaris*
Eastern painted turtle	*Chrysemys picta picta*
Florida chorus frog	*Pseudacris nigrita verrucosa*
Four-striped skink	*Eumeces tetragrammus*
Gopher tortoise	*Gopherus polyphemus*
Greek tortoise	*Testudo graeca*
Green tree frog	*Hyla cinerea cinerea*
Hermann's tortoise	*Testudo hermanni*
Iguana	*Iguana iguana*
Japanese newt	*Molge pyrrhogastra*
Leaf-toed gecko	*Sphaerodactylus xantii*
Leopard gecko	*Eublephorus macularis*
Little green toad	*Bufo debilis*
Long-toed salamander	*Ambystoma macrodactylum*
Madagascan day gecko	*Phelsuma lineata*
Malayan house gecko	Hemidactylus sp.
Marbled salamander	*Ambystoma opacum*

Mediterranean gecko	Hemidactylus sp.
Mobile turtle	*Pseudemys floridana mobilensis*
Mole salamander	*Ambystoma talpoideum*
Monarch's gecko	*Gekko monarchus*
Moorish gecko	*Tarentola mauretanica*
Mountain skink	*Eumeces callicephalus*
Northern chuckwalla	*Sauromalus obesus*
Northern diamondback terrapin	*Malaclemys terrapin terrapin*
Oak toad	*Bufo quercicus*
Ornate chorus frog	*Pseudacris ornata*
Pacific tree frog	*Hyla regilla*
Pickerel frog	*Rana palustris*
Purple salamander	*Gryinophilus porphyriticus*
Ravine salamander	*Plethodon richmondi*
Red-backed salamander	*P. cinerus*
Red-eared turtle	*Pseudemys scripta elegans*
Red-footed tortoise	*Geochelone carbonaria*
Red salamander	*Pseudotriton ruber*
Red-spotted newt	*Triturus viridescens*
Reef gecko	*Sphaerodactylus notatus*
Ricard's frog	*Eleutherodactylus ricordii planirostris*
Round-toed gecko	*Sphaerodactylus elegans*
Sawback turtle	*Graptemys pseudogeographica kohnii*
Short-horned toad	*Phrynosoma douglassii douglassii*
Short-lined skink	*Eumeces brevilineatus*
Side blotch uta	*Uta stansburiana stansbariana*
Southern fence lizard	*Sceloporus undulatus*
Southern painted turtle	*Chrysemys picta dorsalis*
Southern toad	*Bufo terrestris*
Spadefoot toad	*Scaphiopus holbrookii holbrookii*
Spiny-tailed iguana	*Ctenosaura pectinita*
Spotted turtle	*Clemmys guttata*
Spring peeper	*Hylidae crucifer crucifer*
Striped red-tailed skink	*Eumeces egregius*
Tiger salamander	*Ambystoma tigrinum*
Tokay gecko	*Gekko gecko*

Water skink	Lygosoma
Wellers salamander	*Plethodon welleri*
Western banded gecko	*Coleonyx variegatus*
Western box turtle	*Terrapene ornata*
Western collared lizard	*Crotaphytus collaris baileyi*
Western fence lizard	*Sceloporus occidentalis biseriatus*
Western newt	Taricha
Western painted turtle	*Chrysemys picta belli*
Western skink	*Eumeces skiltonianus*
Western toad	*Bufo cognatus*
Western tree frog	*Hyla versicolor chrysoscelis*
Wood frog	*Rana sylvatica sylvatica*
Wood turtle	*Bufo woodhousii woodhoussii*
Woodhouses's toad	*Plethodon dorsalis*
Zigzag salamander	*Clemmys insculpta*

BIBLIOGRAPHY: Reptiles and Amphibians

A Field Guide to Western Reptiles and Amphibians, Robert C. Stebbins, Houghton Mifflin, Boston, 1966

A Field Guide to the Reptiles and Amphibians of the Eastern U.S. and Canada, Roger Conant, Houghton Mifflin, Boston, 1958

Frogs and Toads as Pets, Dr. Herbert R. Axelrod, TFH Publications, Jersey City, N.J., 1970

Geckos as Pets, Ray Pauley, TFH Publications, Jersey City, N.J., 1966

Handbook of Lizards, Hobart M. Smith, Cornell University Press, Ithaca, N.Y., 1967

Handbook of Frogs and Toads, Albert Hazen Wright and Anna Alma Wright, Cornell University Press, Ithaca, N.Y., 1967

Living Reptiles of the World, Karl P. Schmidt and Robert F. Inger, Doubleday & Co., Garden City, N.Y., 1957

Reptiles as Pets, Paul Villiard, Doubleday & Co., Garden City, N.Y., 1969

The Life of Reptiles (two volumes), Angus Bellairs, Universe Natural History Series, Universe Books, New York, 1970

Turtles, Robert J. Church, TFH Publications, Jersey City, N.J., 1963

Your Terrarium, Mervin F. Roberts, TFH Publications, Jersey City, N.J., 1963

Plants

All About Miniature Plants and Gardens, Indoors and Out, Bernice
Brilmayer, Doubleday & Co., Garden City, N.Y., 1963
Bottle Gardens and Fern Cases, Anne Ashberry, Hodder & Stoughton,
Ltd., London, 1964
Cacti and Succulents, Editors with Jack Kramer, Lane Publishing,
Menlo Park, Calif., 1969
Forests of Liliput, John H. Balland, Prentice-Hall, Englewood Cliffs,
N.J., 1971
Gardens Under Glass, Jack Kramer, Simon & Schuster, New York, 1970
Miniature Plants Indoors and Out, Jack Kramer, Charles Scribner's
Sons, New York, 1971
Nature in Miniature, Birger Richard Headstrom, Alfred A. Knopf, New
York, 1968

Where to Buy Plants

Alberts & Merkel Bros, Inc. P.O. Box 537 Boynton Beach, Fla. 334335	Miniature orchids; tropical plants
Arthur Eames Allgrove North Wilmington, Mass. 01887	All kinds of vivarium plants
Hausermans Orchids Box 363 Elmhurst, Ill. 60218	Miniature orchids
Lamb Nurseries E. 101 Sharp Ave. Spokane, Wash. 99202	Wildflowers
Lounsberry Gardens P.O. Box 135 Oakford, Ill. 62673	Wildflowers
Merry Gardens Camden, Me. 04843	All kinds of miniature plants
Mincemoyer Nursery Rt. 5, Box 379 Jackson, N.J. 08527	Wildflowers

George W. Park Seed Co.   All kinds of miniature plants
P.O. Box 31
Greenwood, S.C. 29646

Clyde Robin   Wildflowers
P.O. Box 2091
Castro Valley, Calif. 94546

Tropical Paradise Greenhouses   All kinds of miniature plants
8825 W. 79th St.
Overland Pk., Kans. 66200